Prayer Helper

Derbrah Ajike-King

Prayer Helper

ISBN-13: 978-1537558370

ISBN-10: 1537558374

E-Book ASIN: B01M2WZSLU

All scriptures taken from the King James Version (KJV)
Public Domain

Book cover – Ola Kate

Dedication

*To everyone
who has prayed for me,
prayed with me
and
inspired me to pray.*

Acknowledgements

Our heavenly Father for the awesome privilege to come boldly into His presence and ask in the name of Jesus, and also to receive by faith.

Our gracious Savior for His unending love wherewith He saved us and made us right with God.

Our glorious Comforter for choosing to live within us and help us daily to please God.

My nuclear and extended family members for inspiring me to pray.

Every believer, especially, ministers who instructed, encouraged and empowered me to pray. Thank you!

About This Book

This book is to help anyone having challenges praying or anyone willing to expand prayer options and grow in prayer. God wants His people to pray, especially in these last days, we HAVE to PRAY! There are many types of prayer and this book gives a primer in the different prayer types. While one can pray in the heart, and or in the mind, Yeshua (Hebrew name for Jesus) told us to "say" when we pray (Luke 11:2), so use your mouth, use your words and your voice, and say, when you pray.

Prayer Helper is divided into 5 parts, and contains many 5-minute primers. It is a self-help book so use it regularly! Even when you don't feel like praying, merely stating a few of the prayers will usher you into the prayer mood. Let this tool be a helper to you and for you, and share it with others who may need it.

All the prayers are made to God the Father in the name of God the Son (written as Jesus or Yeshua – the Hebrew pronunciation) and are inspired by God the Holy Spirit. *Prayer Helper* will positively influence and impact your life so be prepared for godly power, peace and joy as you faithfully pray.

Adonai bless and keep you as you yield to His Spirit to pray in the name of Yeshua. Amein.

Table of Contents

Matthew 9: 15 "And Jesus said unto them, Can the children of the bridechamber mourn, as long as the bridegroom is with them? but the days will come, when the bridegroom shall be taken from them, and then shall they fast."

Mark 2:20 "But the days will come, when the bridegroom shall be taken away from them, and then shall they fast in those days."

Luke 5:35 "But the days will come, when the bridegroom shall be taken away from them, and then shall they fast in those days."

Types of Prayer

Praying is defined as talking to God and many have added, that it involves also allowing Him to talk back to you.

There are many types of prayer, the first is the *Prayer of Praise* also called *Thanksgiving Prayer* – This is usually the beginning and closing of every prayer. Here, we praise God, in Jesus name for Who He is, what He has done, what He is doing and for what He will do.

Prayer of Petition – This is also called *the Prayer of Faith*. Here we ask God in the name of Yeshua for a particular thing, believe that God will do the thing while we are asking, and are confident that the prayer is answered.

Warfare Prayer – Also called the *Prayer of Taking Authority*, and/or the *Prayer of Binding and Loosing*. This type of prayer utilizes the name of Jesus Christ and other weapons of the believer to overcome evil spirits and their evil work. One must pray with determination and spiritual aggression, it is spiritual battle.

Prayer of Agreement – This is when two or more Christians unite together to pray on a prayer point. It is a very powerful form of prayer and it makes tremendous power available. It only works if all parties are in agreement so there must be no doubting.

Prayer of Supplication – This is like the prayer of faith but it carries a sense of waiting on God, tarrying in prayer, seeking God's face. One isn't just asking God to do something and thanking Him, one is "pleading" with God as it were. A good example is how our Lord Jesus Christ prayed in the Garden of Gethsemane. Usually with this type of prayer, the focus is one prayer point. This type of prayer is usually used alongside the prayer of intercession.

Prayer with the Spirit – This is also called *praying in (or with) the Spirit or praying in (or with) other tongues.* This type of prayer enables the believer to pray the mysteries of God and pray according to the will of God. It generates spiritual power and edifies the believer. It is very essential in spiritual battle and achieving victory. It is prayed with all types of prayer. If you are not yet filled, pray the prayer on page 13 and you'll be filled through faith in God's word.

Prayer of Intercession – This is when one prays for another person or a group of people or even an animal or a thing.

Confessional Prayer – also called *Prophetic Prayer*, this is when the word of God is prophesied in a situation and/or upon a person. Personalizing God's promises opens a new realm of benefits to the believer. Get my book – *Living Words of Prayer* for over 217 personalized promises of God's word in a daily fashion.

Prayer of Salvation: This is usually called the sinner's prayer. This is a prayer everyone prays to become born again. It is simply stating one's faith in the Lordship of Yeshua (Jesus). If you are not yet saved and would like to be saved, pray the prayer. It is very important that one is saved. Without salvation, one cannot access righteousness which means a right standing with God. This is only done through faith in the resurrection of Jesus Christ and declaring Him as Lord. See the next two pages for an example of this prayer.

These are the basic types of prayers and they can be prayed at any time of the day. God loves it when we call on Him, so **pray**!

Part 1 - General Prayers

These general prayers are for everyone. It outlines the basic prayer types. Everyone needs to be saved and filled with the Holy Spirit. Everyone must offer sacrifices of praise and thanksgiving to God.

Every Christian should fast and Christians should join together to pray the prayer of agreement. There is a daily prayer which incorporates all the different types of prayer in this section.

Luke 18:1;
"And he (Jesus) spake a parable
unto them to this end,
that men ought always to pray,
and not to faint;"

Emphasis mine.

Salvation Prayer

Salvation – this is an important thing to note. Are you saved? Before you can pray efficiently, you need to be saved. This is very important! What is salvation?

Salvation is the process by which a person receives eternal life. The Bible is based on the Holy God Who created mankind in His image and likeness (Genesis 1:26-27). He gave mankind a command which was disobeyed, leading to mankind's loss of God's holiness and mankind's acquisition of the sinful nature (Genesis 2:17, 3:6, 15-24, Romans 5:12).

God loved man and paved a way of escape for man from sin and its consequences. He sent His only begotten Son; Jesus Christ (Yeshua Mashiach) to pay the debt of sin which is death. Jesus went to Hell (Hades) instead of man and rose again on the third day for man's justification (Romans 5:15-19, 2 Corinthians 5:14). Jesus was not born with a sinful nature like every human being, so He qualified to be the propitiation for the sins of the world (John 1:29, 2 Corinthians 5:21).

God will forgive the sin, and consequences of sin (which is mainly spiritual death) of anyone who believes in his or her heart that Jesus rose from the dead for his or her sins and confesses with his or her mouth that Jesus is his or her Lord (Romans 10:9-10). This is why those who believe in Jesus, have everlasting life.

"For God so loved the world, that he gave his only begotten Son, that whosoever believeth in him should not perish, but have everlasting life." – John 3:16.

It's like an equation; belief in the heart that God raised Jesus from the dead plus confession with the mouth that Jesus is Lord equals eternal salvation. Your faith in the sacrifice that Jesus made for you and your willingness to make Him the Lord of Your life, activates God's justification for you.

So if you are ready to commit your life to Jesus Christ, and receive eternal life, pray the following;

According to God's word, I believe in my heart that God raised Jesus from the dead and I confess with my mouth that Jesus is my Lord, therefore I am saved. Thank You Lord for saving me in Jesus name. Amein.

Thanksgiving Prayer

Blessed are You o Lord our God, King of the universe, Creator of heaven and earth and all therein. You are great and worthy to be praised. You are God and there is none like You. You are good and full of mercy.

You are the LORD, The LORD God, merciful and gracious, longsuffering, and abundant in goodness and truth. You keep mercy for thousands, and forgive iniquity, transgression and sin, You are the Merciful One, You are God, the Faithful God that keepeth covenant and mercy. You are He that dwells in the third heaven, You are He that sits upon the throne, You are He that dwells among Your people, amein, blessings and glory, wisdom, thanksgiving and honor, power and might be unto You Lord, forever and ever, amein.

Father, You said "Whoso offereth praise glorifieth me, and to him that ordereth *his* conversation *aright* will I show the salvation of God." Let my praise glorify You as I praise. I will bless the LORD at all times: his praise *shall* continually *be* in my mouth. I have tasted and seen that the LORD *is* good, indeed, blessed *is* the man *that* trusteth in him.

I fear You LORD, I am Your saint, and *there is* no want to them that fear You. LORD, You are my strength and song, and You have become my salvation. I will praise thee: for You have heard me, and You are my salvation.

Father, I give You thanks for You are good and Your mercies endure forever. I join with the 24 elders and the four living creatures and holy angels in heaven and cry Holy, Holy, Holy, Lord God Almighty, Who was, Who is, and is to come. For You are good, You are the only One good, You alone, o Lord, for Your loving kindness endures forever. I praise You, I worship You, I adore You, I glorify You, I bless You, I ascribe to You the greatness, the majesty, the excellence, the honor, the riches, the blessing, the wealth, the glory, the accolade, the gratitude, the praise, the worthiness, the power, the pomp, the priority, the preference, the royalty, the purity, and the potency, I extol You, O Perfect One.

You are highly lifted up and glorious. You are the only God, You are the Almighty One. You are the One Who dwells by the sides of the north, You are the Holy One of Israel, You are all powerful, all-knowing, all-present and all-wise. Thank You for Your bountiful mercies upon my life.

Thank You for Your faithfulness, thank You for Your loving kindness, thank You for Your goodness, thank You for Your unending love. Thank You for Your steadfast love, Your grace, Your favor and Your power in Jesus mighty name I praise.

Exodus 34:6-7, Deuteronomy 4:31, 7:9, Psalm 34:1 and 8, 48:1-2, 50:23, 118:1,14, 21 and 29, Revelation 4:8-11, 7:12.

Prayer to be filled with the Spirit

Heavenly Father, thank You for the infilling of the Holy Spirit with the evidence of speaking with other tongues. According to Your word, the promise of the gift of the Holy Spirit is for me as a believer in the Lordship of Jesus Christ, therefore heavenly Father, I ask for the infilling of Your Spirit that I may be a witness for you and also speak in tongues as your Spirit gives me utterance. Thank You Lord that in keeping with Your word, which says that everyone that asks receives, I therefore receive the infilling of the Holy Spirit with the evidence of speaking with other tongues now in Yeshua's holy name. Thank You Father for answering my prayer in Jesus name I pray, amein.

Mark 16:17, Acts 1:8, 2:4, Luke 11:13, and Matthew 7:7

After praying this prayer in faith, one of two things usually happens; the tongue language changes and the believer begins to say words that sound strange or the believer hears strange words in his/her head or ears and has to choose to say those words. The Holy Spirit will not force Your mouth open, you must speak them forth.

Tongues are a prayer language and they are not learned or understood by the mind! They are however very powerful in praying the perfect will of the Father and praying with the assistance of the Holy Spirit. Therefore, pray always [1Corinthians 14:2, 14, Romans 8:26].

Example of Petition Prayer

Heavenly Father, Thank You for the privilege of calling You Father because of Your Son, Yeshua. Thank You for Your word that says in Matthew 7:7-9 to ask and receive, seek and find and knock and have the door opened. Your word also states in Mark 11:24 that if I believe that I receive whatever I ask you in prayer, I shall receive, therefore, this moment I ask You to .... (place your petition request here) in the name of Jesus.

In agreement with Your word, I believe that I receive that which I have asked for and I give You thanks, honor, glory and adoration, in Jesus name.

Galatians 4:1-6, Mark 11:24, Matthew 7:7-9, Hebrews 11:1-6 and 1 John 5:14-15.

Prayer of Supplication

Most High God and Father of our Lord Jesus Christ, I come boldly into Your presence through the blood of Jesus and I ask that You .... (place your supplication request here) in the name of Jesus. Father, remember the fact that I have kissed the Son and show Yourself strong in my behalf. Help me access Your blessings for my life. Whatever I need to do, whatever I need to say, in order for the answers to my prayers to come to pass, Father, reveal to me and help me to do it in Yeshua's name.

Father, regarding this issue, I ask for Your intervention. King of all kings, Lord of all lords, Prince of peace, omnipotent One, Omnipresent One, Omniscient One, help me in the name of Jesus. Remember the blood of Yeshua that was shed on my behalf and save me. Let Your word be honored in my life, let Your praise continually be on my lips, deliver me o Lord in Jesus name.

Abba, send forth Your saving power and rescue me. I have no one else but You, I need no One else but You. Let me not be ashamed, let not my enemies triumph over me. Let not the mockers prevail o Adonai, let the pleasure that Jesus gives to You quicken Your deliverance power to me.

You are the Almighty One, You are the King of all the earth, You alone are God, and I worship You, I praise You, I look up to You. Thank You Father for hearing my cry in the life-saving name of Jesus, Amein.

Philippians 4:6-7, 1 Kings 8:28-59, 2 Chronicles 6:19, 21, 24, 39 and 33:13, Psalms 2:10, 6:9,30:8, 55:1, 119:170 and 142:1, Jeremiah, 31:9, Daniel 6:11 and 9:3, 18 and 20, Zechariah 12. 10, Acts 1:14, Ephesians 6:18, Matthew 3:17, 1 Timothy 2:5, 5:5, and Hebrews 5:7.

Prayer of Forgiveness of Sins

The only good God and Father of the Lord Jesus Christ, I am so grateful that I belong to You. Father You are holy and Your eyes cannot behold iniquity. You want me to come boldly to Your throne of grace to obtain mercy and find grace to help in the time of need so I come boldly to You in the name of Jesus.

According to Your provision in 1 John 1:9, I confess my sins to You, for if I confess my sins, You are faithful and just to forgive me my sins, and to cleanse me from all unrighteousness in Jesus name. I confess my sin of .... (place sin here). [If you don't remember all the sins you've done, then say this - *I confess all the sins I have said, heard, seen, touched, smelled, sensed, tasted, eaten, thought, imagined, envisioned, drawn, written and done in Jesus name.*]

Thank You Father that the blood of Yeshua cleanses me from all sin and I am blessed because my transgression is forgiven. I give You glory, honor and adoration in the name of Jesus, amin.

---

1 Corinthians 6:20, Habakkuk 1:13, Hebrews 4:16, John 15:16, Colossians 1:14 and Psalm 32:1.

Prayer to Fast

Heavenly Father, thank You for the grace and honor to call upon You in the name of Jesus. You desire that Your people fast and pray to set the captives free as evidenced in Isaiah 58:6-12. You want Your people to fast and pray to loosen the bands of wickedness, undo the heavy burdens, let the oppressed go free, and break every yoke. Thank You for helping me fast that I may cast out evil spirits that do not go out except by prayer and fasting in Yeshua's name.

Father, help me by Your Spirit, to fulfill the type of fast that You have chosen in Jesus name. Lord, help me to pray being led by Your Spirit and Your word in the name of Yeshua. Help me also to walk in godly love, to deal my bread to the hungry, to bring the poor that are cast out to my house, to cover the naked and take care of my relatives.

Adonai, Your word says that when I do this, then shall my light break forth as the morning, and my health shall spring forth speedily, and my righteousness shall go before me and Your glory shall be my reward in Jesus name. Then shall I call, and You shall answer, I will cry and You will say, "Here I am."

If I take away from me the yoke, the putting forth of the finger, and speaking vanity, if I draw out my soul to the hungry, and satisfy the afflicted soul, then shall my light rise in obscurity, and my darkness be as the noon day in the name of Yeshua. Thank You LORD for You will guide me continually, and satisfy my soul in drought, and make fat my bones, and I shall be like a watered garden, and like a spring of water, whose waters fail not in Jesus name.

21

Help me Lord when I fast, to be not as the hypocrites, who wear a sad countenance, disfiguring their faces, that they may appear unto men to fast, but help me to anoint my head, wash my face, that I appear not unto men to fast, but unto You Father Who are in secret, and You Father, Who sees in secret, shall reward me openly in Yeshua's name.

Abba, as I minister to You and fast, let me hear the voice of the Holy Spirit clearly and help me to be obedient in Jesus name. I thank You Lord that as I fast and beseech You, You will be entreated of me in the name of Yeshua, You will help me Lord to approve myself as Your minister even in fasting, in the name of Jesus, amin.

Matthew 6:16-18, 17:21, Acts 13:2, Ezra 8:23 and 2 Corinthians 6:4.

Prayer of Agreement

Heavenly Father, Your word says in Matthew 18:19 that if two of us shall agree on earth as touching anything that we shall ask, it shall be done for us of You Father Who are in heaven, in Jesus name. Therefore Lord, according to Your word, _____ (put your partner's name) and I come to You regarding _____ (state your prayer focus) and we touch and agree that _____ (make your request) in the name of Yeshua.

We have confidence in Your word that our request is granted in Jesus name. Thank You Lord for answering our prayer in the name of Yeshua.

Amein.

Prayer to Forgive Others

Read the following scriptures – John 1:12, 2 Corinthians 5:21, 1 John 1:7, Colossians 3:13, Ephesians 4:31-32, Romans 12:17-21, Matthew 6:12, 14-15,18:21-35, Luke 6:27-37 1 Peter 3:9, Mark 11:25-26, and Philippians 4:4.

All merciful God, I come to You humbly and in gratitude. Thank You for making me Your son in Christ Jesus and for giving me righteousness through His blood. You desire that I forgive those who hurt me, even when I do not feel like it, so Lord in obedience to Your word, I forgive .... (place the person's name here) in Jesus name.

I remember Your grace towards me Lord, so I chose to forgive this wrong and free .... (place the person's name here) of their wrong in the name of Yeshua.

I remove bitterness and pain from my heart by choice, empowered by Your Spirit and the blood of Jesus and I chose to remember this hurt and pain, no more and continue my life's journey rejoicing in You always, Lord, in the name of Jesus, amin.

Daily Morning Prayer

My heavenly Father, thank You for Your love for me. Thank You for waking me up to a new day. Your word says, today is a day that You have made, therefore I will rejoice and be glad in it, and I declare that today is Your created day so I shall rejoice in You today in Jesus name. Help me Father to go through this day with plenty of gratitude and a godly attitude. Your word says that You keep in perfect peace, they, whose minds are stayed on you, help me to keep my mind on You, on Your word, on Your love, that I may be in perfect peace in Yeshua's name.

Father, I thank You that I am Your workmanship in Christ Jesus, created for good works that You predestined for me to work in them, help me to achieve the quota of good works You predestined me to accomplish for this day in Jesus name. You desire Father, that all men repent and come to the knowledge of the truth, help me to share the truth of Your word with those that need to hear it from me today in Yeshua's name.

I praise You Father that as many as are led by Your Spirit are Your sons, help me to be yielded to the Holy Spirit today in all I think, say and do. Your word also declares that You Lord will bless the righteous and with favor will You enclose the righteous as a shield, I proclaim, that I am blessed of You, Father and Your favor encloses me as a shield in Jesus name. I meet Your favor in every place I go in Yeshua's name.

I take authority over the evil one today and decree and declare that no weapon fashioned against me shall prosper and every tongue that rises up against me shall be condemned in the name of Yeshua. This is my heritage as the servant of the LORD, and my vindication comes from You, Lord.

I pray for everyone alive on the earth today, I ask that You will help them to recognize that they were not created for themselves but that they were created to please You Lord. Place the perfect laborer of the gospel in the lives of every boy, girl, woman and/man that is not yet saved today. Let Your laborers share Your good news with them and let them have an understanding heart in Jesus name. I pray that the light of the gospel of Christ will shine into the hearts of those not saved, and Satan's power over their minds be broken in the name of Yeshua.

I pray for leaders of all homes, firms, towns, states and nations and ask that they would make wise and godly choices today in Jesus name. Thank You also Lord, for helping our ministers, leaders of Your church worldwide, to stand strong in You in Jesus name.

I confess that I am blessed going out and I am blessed coming in, in the mighty name of Jesus. Thank You Abba for answering my prayer, in Yeshua's mighty name I pray. Amein.

Psalm 118:24, Isaiah 26:3, Ephesians 2:10, 1 Timothy 2:4, 2 Timothy 4:2, Romans 8:14, Psalm 5:12, Isaiah 54:17, Deuteronomy 28:6, Revelation 4:11.

Birthday Prayer

Thank You Lord for another year, I am grateful for Your grace that has kept me and will continually keep me in Yeshua's name. I declare that like Asher, I am blessed, I have favor with God and man, I dip my feet in oil in Jesus name. My shoes are like iron and brass, and as my days are, so shall my strength be in the name of Yeshua.

There is none like You Lord, the God of Jeshurun, Who rides upon the heaven, and Your excellency on the sky, You Lord, are my help. Eternal God, You are my refuge, and underneath me are Your everlasting arms, Lord, You shall thrust out the enemy from before me and declare "Destroy them" in Jesus name. I, Your Israel, shall then dwell in safety alone, I shall have more than enough and my heavens shall drop down dew in the name of Yeshua.

I rejoice in You Lord today and I am glad, yes I am happy, for You have saved me, You are the shield of my help, and the Sword of my excellency in the name of Jesus! My enemies shall be found to be liars and I shall tread upon their high places in Yeshua's name. My bread shall be fat and I shall yield royal dainties in the name of Jesus.

I proclaim that like Joseph, I am a fruitful bough, even a fruitful bough by a well; whose branches run over the wall. I shall increase in Yeshua's name. Adonai shall cause my glory to be like the firstling of the bullock, and my horns, like the horns of unicorns, with them, I shall push the people together to the ends of the earth and I shall receive help when I need it in the name of Jesus!

My land is blessed of You, LORD, I receive the precious things of heaven, for the dew, and for the deep that couches beneath, the precious fruits brought forth by the sun, and for the precious things put forth by the moon, and for the chief things of the ancient mountains, and for the precious things of the lasting hills, and for the precious things of the earth and fulness thereof, and for the good will of him that dwelt in the bush in Jesus name. The blessing comes upon my head, on top of my head in the name of Yeshua.

The archers may have sorely grieved me, and shot at me, and hated me, but my bow abides in strength, and the arms of my hands are made strong by the hands of the mighty God of Jacob, even the Shepherd, the Stone of Israel, even by the God of Yeshua, Who helps me; and by the Almighty, Who blesses me with blessings of heaven above, blessings of the deep that lies under, blessings of the breasts, and of the womb in the name of Jesus! I am blessed of Elshaddai above the blessings of my progenitors unto the utmost bound of the everlasting hills, Adonai's blessings shall be on my head and on my crown in the name of Yeshua.

Like Yeshua did when He was physically on the earth, I grow, and wax strong in spirit, filled with wisdom: and the grace of God is upon me, yes, I increase in wisdom and stature, and in favour with God and man in Yeshua's name. Amein.

Deuteronomy 33:25-29, Genesis 49:20,22-26 and Luke 2:40, 52

Part 2 - Personal Prayers

This section deals with prayers every Christian has prayed, will or should pray at least once in their Christian walk. Every child of God should desire to grow spiritually, overcome hindrances, bear much spiritual fruit, redeem the time, and fulfill their prophetic destiny.

Pray these prayers with sincerity and all seriousness. Pray in faith trusting our Lord to answer your prayers, for He wants His children to experience all that He has for them. Pray, knowing that God will always love you. Pray when you feel like it and when you don't feel like it. Pray because you know prayer works! Pray when you're depressed, discouraged or sad. Pray when you're excited, happy or sad. Pray, because the Father wants your joy to be full!

As you pray these prayers, things will shift in the spirit realm and your physical reality will change. Adonai will help you pray as you choose to. Blessings!

"Hitherto have ye asked nothing in my name: ask, and ye shall receive, that your joy may be full."
- John 16:24.

Be careful for nothing; but in everything by prayer and supplication with thanksgiving let your requests be made known unto God.
- Philippians 4:6.

Praying always with all prayer and supplication in the Spirit, and watching thereunto with all perseverance and supplication for all saints;
- Ephesians 6:18.

Prayer to Grow Spiritually

My heavenly Father, I thank You for the grace to belong to You. Thank You for Your love and Your grace in Jesus Christ. Thank You that You delight to fellowship with me and I can boldly come into Your presence in the name of Jesus.

Father, I desire to increase in knowledge and fellowship with You daily. Help me to grow spiritually, for eternal life is to know You and Yeshua Whom You have sent. Let my knowledge of You grow unhindered for they that know their God shall be strong and do exploits.

Lead me Abba, by Your Spirit and Your word to redeem the time and spend quality time with You, with Your word, meditating and yielding my life and my members to Your will in the name of Yeshua. Let Your word be in my heart and on my lips all through the day in the name of Jesus. Help me to keep my mind on You, so You can keep me in perfect peace in Yeshua's name.

Thank You Baba, that I will be dedicated to seek Your face and obey Your voice in Jesus name. Thank You that I will be bold to declare Your Lordship and good news to others in the name of Yeshua. Thank You for helping me to move from one level of glory to the other in Your grace, in Jesus name I pray. Amein.

Deuteronomy 32:9, 1 John 1:7, 4:4,19, Ephesians 2:8,5:16, Hebrews 4:16, John 17:3, Daniel 11:32b, Romans 12:1-2, Joshua 1:8, Isaiah 26:3 and 2 Corinthians 3:18.

Prayer to Overcome Hindrances

Abba, our Hope and Strength, our Defender and Fortress, I praise and adore You. I glorify You and magnify Your holy name, for You are good and Your mercies endure forever. Thank You Lord that it is the evil one that has come to steal, kill and destroy, but Yeshua has come to give me life and life more abundantly. I ask Lord that You help me overcome every hindrance the enemy places across my path in Jesus name. Grant me Lord Your wisdom to be protected from deception and teach me Your way so I'll walk in Your truth, unite my heart to fear Your name so that I will not be rebellious in the name of Yeshua.

Help me Father, to keep Your word active in my life by declaring it all through the day and to teach those around me as Your word dictates, for if I diligently keep all Your commandments to do them, to love the LORD my God, to walk in all Your ways, and to cleave unto You, then You, LORD will drive out all these nations (hindrances) from before me and I shall possess greater and mightier nations than myself, I shall perform the good works pre-ordained by God for me in Jesus name. Every place whereon the soles of my feet shall tread shall be mine in Yeshua's name, and I will accomplish my godly goals overcoming every hindrance. There shall no man be able to stand before me, for You, the LORD my God shall lay the fear of me and the dread of me upon all the land that I shall tread upon, that is, upon all my hindrances in Jesus name. I choose the blessing You've set before me Lord, the blessing of obeying Your word in Yeshua's name.

I praise You Adonai Tz'Vaot (Lord of hosts) for You have strengthened the bars of my gates and I am fortified with Your word, my children are blessed and You make peace in my life and cause me to be at peace with others in Jesus name.

You supply my every need according to Your riches in glory by Yeshua and show me Your word, statutes and judgments in the name of Jesus. You Lord have brought me, in Christ, out of darkness and the shadow of death, and You have broken the bands of my attackers in sunder and translated me into the kingdom of Your dear Son. I praise You LORD for Your goodness, mercy, grace, and Your wonderful works to me, for You have broken the gates of brass, and cut the bars of iron in sunder.

According to Your word, no weapon formed against me shall prosper and every tongue that rises up against me shall be condemned in Yeshua's name. Lord of hosts, You disappoint the devices of the crafty, so that their hands cannot perform their enterprise, and take the wise in their own craftiness, and the counsel of the froward is carried headlong. These hindrance creators shall meet with darkness in the daytime, and grope in the noonday as in the night in Jesus name.

Thank You Abba, that You save the poor from the sword, and from the mouth, and hands of the mighty. I am grateful Lord that every hindrance in my life is overcome in Yeshua's mighty name. Amein.

John 10:10, Deuteronomy 11:18-27, Psalm 86:11, 107:14-15, 147:13-17, Philippians 4:19, Job 5:12-15, Isaiah 54:17 and Colossians 1:13.

Prayer to Bear Much Spiritual Fruit

Abba in heaven, thank You for saving my soul through the blood of Jesus Christ, Your only begotten Son. I pray that I live a fruitful Christian life in Jesus name. Help me Lord to bear much spiritual fruit by abiding in You for Father, You are the Husbandman, Yeshua is the True Vine, and I am Your branch. Purge me so that I will continually bear fruit in the name of Yeshua.

Baba, help me to abide in Jesus, remove from me, anything that will not cause me to abide in You in Jesus name. Cause me to dwell upon Your word, and for Your word to dwell in me, that I shall ask what I will, and it shall be done unto me in the name of Yeshua. Father, be glorified in my life, for when I bear much fruit, You are glorified and I am a disciple of Jesus. Yeshua has chosen me, and ordained me, that I should go and bring forth fruit, and that my fruit should remain, that whatsoever I shall ask of the Father in Jesus name, He may give it to me.

I lift up my eyes, and look on the fields, for they are white already to harvest, and by Your grace, Lord, I reap the harvest and receive wages and gather fruit unto life eternal in the name of Yeshua. Thank You Papa that both he that sows and he that reaps rejoice together, so I love other Christians and join with them to preach the good news and the evil one cannot overcome us in Jesus name.

I praise You and worship You Lord that I bear much spiritual fruit in Yeshua's name. Amin.

John 4:35-36,15:1-8, 16-17, and 1 John 3:14.

Prayer to Redeem the Time

My Father in heaven, I worship You and exalt You for You are good and Your mercies endure forever. Your word declares Lord, that to everything there is a season, and a time to every purpose under the heaven, help me Lord to know the times and seasons of my life that You have set for me and that I yield to Your plan for my life in Jesus name.

I trust in You LORD, and declare that You are my God, and my times are in Your hand. You will deliver me from the hand of my enemies and from them that persecute me in the name of Yeshua. Help me Abba to walk in wisdom toward them that are without, redeeming the time, and let my speech be always with grace, seasoned with salt, that I know how ye ought to answer every man in Jesus name.

Adonai, help me to determine to walk circumspectly, not as fools, but as wise, redeeming the time, because the days are evil in Yeshua's name. Lord You have made of one blood, all nations of men, and we are Your offspring, help me Lord to properly discern the times appointed that I should seek You in Jesus name.

Thank You Baba for in You I live, and move, and have my being. You will lead me by Your Spirit and Your word to keep my mind on You and speak and act only at Your leading to Your glory in Yeshua's name. I praise You for answered prayers in the name of Jesus. Amein.

Ecclesiastes 3:1, Psalm 31:14-15, Colossians 4:5-6, Ephesians 5:15-16, Acts 17:25-28, Isaiah 26:3 and Romans 8:14.

Prayer to Fulfill Prophetic Destiny

King of glory and Father of the Lord Jesus Christ, I am grateful to You for Your love for me. Thank You for saving my soul and accepting me in Your beloved. Thank You that I belong to You and You are my portion. Father You have made me Your workmanship in Christ Jesus unto good works, which You pre- ordained that I should walk in them. Help me to do those good works You've pre-ordained for me in Jesus name.

Thou art worthy, O Lord, to receive glory and honour and power, for You have created all things, and for Your pleasure they are and were created. I am created for Your pleasure, Lord, that is my prophetic destiny. I ask that I bring You pleasure daily in what I choose, say, see, hear, taste, touch, smell, sense and do, in the name of Yeshua.

Abba, Your word is full of prophecies concerning the body of Christ, Your called out ones, the Ekklesia, of which I am a part, help me Father, to utilize Your prophecies, Your promises to me, to war a good warfare in Jesus name. Lord, help me to hold up faith, and a good conscience and never let it go, standing having done all to stand in the name of Yeshua. Thank You Lord for I fulfill my prophetic destiny in Jesus name. Amein.

Deuteronomy 32:9, Ephesians 2:10, 6:13, Revelation 4:11, 1 Timothy 1:18-19

Prayer to Know God's will and receive God's Wisdom

Adonai Elohim, my Lord and God, I worship You and exalt Your holy name. Thank You heavenly Father, that You love me and care for me, more than I love myself. I am grateful that You created me to bring You pleasure and that I am Your workmanship in Christ Jesus. You said Your sheep hear Your voice and if I lack wisdom I should ask You. Abba, I need to know Your perfect will regarding this .... (place the issue here), show me, lead me, assure me of Your perfect will and unite my heart to obey You fully in the name of Yeshua.

It is written in Your word that concerning Daniel, Shadrach, Meshach and Abednego, that You gave them knowledge and skill in all learning and wisdom, and Daniel had understanding in all visions and dreams. I request in the name of Jesus, that You give me knowledge and skill in all learning and wisdom and that like Daniel, I will have understanding in all visions and dreams.

I ask that I be filled with the knowledge of Your will in all wisdom and spiritual understanding, that I might walk worthy of You Lord unto all pleasing, being fruitful in every good work, and increasing in Your knowledge in Jesus name. I also pray Father that I stand perfect, spiritually mature and complete in all Your will and purpose for my life in the name of Yeshua. Grant me Lord a willing heart to make any change in my life that Your perfect will requires that I make in the name of Jesus.

As your word declares Lord regarding apostle Paul, that You chosen him that he should know Your will, and see You, The Just One, and that he should hear the voice of Your mouth, so have chosen me in Yeshua, help me to know Your will, and see You and to hear the voice of Your mouth in the name of Yeshua. I proclaim that I am not confused or ignorant of Your perfect will for my life Lord, but I am assured of everything willed by God in Jesus name.

Remove from my life Lord, distractions from hearing and seeing You clearly, in the name of Yeshua. Help me Abba to change any mindset that is not according to Your will for my life and strengthen me to break off any relationship that is against Your perfect will for my life in Jesus mighty name. I declare that I am bold and strong to obey You Lord in Yeshua's name.

According to God's word that the path of the just is as the shining light, that shineth more and more unto the perfect day, I confess that regarding .... (state the issue here), my path shines brighter, I understand more clearly what I should do, how I should do it, when I should do it, where I should do it, why I should do it and which steps to take and which steps to shun in the name of Jesus. Thank You Lord for answering my prayer in the name of Yeshua I pray, amein.

Daniel 1:17, 1 John 4:19, Revelation 4:11, Ephesians 2:10, John 10:27, James 1:5, Romans 8:14, Psalm 86:11, Colossians 1:9-10, 4:12, Acts 22:14 and Proverbs 16:3.

Part 3 – Intercession Prayers

And I sought for a man among them, that should make up the hedge, and stand in the gap before me for the land, that I should not destroy it: but I found none.
— Ezekiel 22:30

This section gives assistance for effective intercessory prayers. Remember that the rule for this kind of prayer is faith and consistency. One must continue to stand in the gap! Intercession prayers are not prayers prayed once. One has to pray over and over and over again. The prayers must be continuous and they are very powerful when prayed. We can stop Satan in his tracks with our prayers. Angels of God are deployed when we pray. Problems are fixed when we pray. Prayers really make a huge difference!

There is a 21-day prayer resource for leaders at the city, state and national levels. Take out time to pray daily for your city, state and nation for the next 21-days. It is better to pray than to complain. It is better to pray than to cry. It is better to pray than to be sad. Please pray for someone else.

Intercessory prayers for the body of Christ, Missionaries and 5-fold ministers are also included. There are also resources for friends, family and fiends (meaning of fiend used here is a cruel and wicked person). Pray these prayers from the heart and in faith to God, Who answers prayers and commands us to pray, always.

Please, pray for others, it is a rewarding experience for everyone.

Day 1

The following prayer is based on 1 Timothy 2:1-3, Proverbs 21:1, and Proverbs 14:34. Use it as a start out prayer for today.

Father, I thank You for Your word where we are exhorted to make supplications, prayers, intercessions, and giving of thanks for all men, and especially for kings, and for all that are in authority; that we may lead a quiet and peaceable life in all godliness and honesty, for You consider it good and acceptable.

Lord, I pray for Los Angeles (name the city where you live), California (name the state where you live) and United States of America (name your country), and I ask that you help our leaders to make godly choices in the decisions they make in the name of Yeshua. Turn their hearts after Your will and let righteousness reign in their professional lives.

Grant unto our leaders Your wisdom and Your grace Lord, to choose wisely and promote goodwill, in Jesus name. Amein.

Day 2

Here is a start out prayer based on Psalm 2:4-5 and Proverbs 14:16.

Heavenly Father, thank You for Your faithfulness in our lives. Thank You for Your mercies and greatness in Jesus name.

Lord we place the city of Los Angeles (name the city where you live), the state of California (name the state where you live) and the nation of the United States of America (name your country) in Your hands. Help us, help our leaders to uphold the way of righteousness and shun evil in Jesus name.

The heathen rage against us o Lord, but we trust in You, "that You, that sitteth in the heavens shall laugh, You Lord shall have our enemies in derision. You shall speak unto them in Your wrath, and vex them in Your sore displeasure.

Thank You Father for loving us and for keeping us in the name of Yeshua. Amin.

Day 3

Here is a start out prayer based on Psalm 124:1, 4-6 and Isaiah 44: 25.

Eternal Rock of ages, we glorify You and praise Your holy Name. Thank You Lord for Your goodness in our lives. If it had not been the Lord on our side, where would we be? Blessed are You Lord, Who has not given us as a prey to the teeth of the enemy. Our soul is escaped as a bird out of the snare of the fowlers, the snare is broken, and we are escaped. Halleluyah to Your name Father, in Jesus name.

Lord we hand over the city of Los Angeles (name the city where you live), the state of California (name the state where you live) and the nation of the United States of America (name your country) unto You. Overshadow us with Your love and mercy and quicken our souls and spirits to obey Your word in the name of Yeshua.

Adonai Tz'vaot, You are the One that frustrates the tokens of the liars, and makes diviners mad, You turn wise men backward, and make their knowledge foolish. Lord, let every evil intended against our cities, states and country be turned around in Jesus name.

We declare that our help is in the name of the Lord, who made heaven and earth. We rest in Your faithfulness Abba. Thank You for Your love in the name of Yeshua. Amein.

Day 4

Here is a start out prayer based on Isaiah 49: 24-25 and Psalm 18: 37-40.

King of glory, Lord of all, we praise You, we worship you, we bless Your holy name. Thank You for Your wonderful love towards us in Jesus name.

Lord we place the city of Los Angeles (name the city where you live), the state of California (name the state where you live) and the nation of the United States of America (name your country) in Your capable hands. Show us Your mercy and turn our hearts unto You in the name of Yeshua.

Your word states that "Shall the prey be taken from the mighty, or the lawful captive delivered? But thus saith the Lord, Even the captives of the mighty shall be taken away, and the prey of the terrible shall be delivered: for I will contend with him that contendeth with thee, and I will save thy children." Father, deliver us and our children from every evil thing that has held us captive in Jesus name.

In keeping with Your word; "I have pursued mine enemies, and overtaken them: neither did I turn again till they were consumed. I have wounded them that they were not able to rise: they are fallen under my feet. For thou hast girded me with strength unto the battle: thou hast subdued under me those that rose up against me. Thou hast also given me the necks of mine enemies; that I might destroy them that hate me.", Father, strengthen us to keep praying until a change manifests.

Encourage and empower Your people to pray and to stand for victory is ours in the name of Yeshua. Thank You Father for answered prayers in Jesus name we pray. Amin.

Day 5

Here is a start out prayer based on Lamentations 3:22-24, Proverbs 29:4 and 14.

Heavenly Father, thank You for Your mercies. It is because of Your mercies that we are not consumed, because Your compassions fail not, they are new every morning and great is Your faithfulness. Lord, You are our portion, our souls say, Lord You are our portion so we hope in You. We are grateful Lord, thank You.

Adonai tz'vaot (Lord of hosts), we seek You regarding the city of Los Angeles (name the city where you live), the state of California (name the state where you live) and the nation of the United States of America (name your country). We ask for leaders that will give our land stability. Your word says "The king gives stability to the land by justice, But a man who takes bribes overthrows it." Let our leaders at every level be men and women who love justice and reject evil in Jesus name.

Father, let our leaders be particularly mindful of the poor, to consider the case of the poor that their thrones may be established for a long time in the name of Yeshua.

Let our leaders commit themselves to alleviating the sufferings of the orphans and the poor, while being mindful that God created all men equal in Jesus name.

Thank You Father for answered prayers in the name of Yeshua, amein.

Day 6

Here is a start out prayer based on Psalm 22:28, Lamentations 3:25-26 and 1 Peter 2:17.

Source of life and Creator of all, we are so blessed to be called Your sons in Christ Jesus. Heavenly Papa, thank You so much for Your unfailingly love for us. Thank You for Your goodness, Your kindness and Your grace in Jesus name.

Lord, we come to You asking that You take over the affairs concerning the city of Los Angeles (name the city where you live), the state of California (name the state where you live) and the nation of the United States of America (name your country). For kingship belongs to You Lord, and You rule over the nations. Rule over us Father, rule over us in the name of Yeshua.

Abba, I ask that You cause Your people across the land to wait upon You. For You are good to them that wait for you, You are good to the soul that seeks You. It is therefore good that a man should both hope and quietly wait for the salvation of Adonai.

Help Your people Lord to obey Your word by honoring all people, loving the brotherhood, fearing You God, and honoring the king. Thank You Baba for answered prayers in Jesus name we pray. Amin.

Day 7

Here is a start out prayer based on Psalm 65:2, 68:1-3 and Romans 13:3-4.

Giver and Maker of Life, we praise You for You are good and You are God! The praise belongs to You o God that answers prayer and unto You shall all flesh come!

We come to You committing the city of Los Angeles (name the city where you live), the state of California (name the state where you live) and the nation of the United States of America (name your country) in Your hands. Let Your plan, purpose and power be done in our lives in the name of Yeshua.

Let God arise, let His enemies be scattered, let them also that hate Him flee before Him. Adonai, as smoke is driven away, so drive them away, as wax melts before the fire, so let the wicked perish at the presence of God in Jesus name. But let the righteous be glad, let them rejoice before God, yes, let them exceedingly rejoice. We rejoice in You o Lord our God for You are good!

Father, we ask that You make our leaders true ministers of You. Let them not be a terror to good works, but to evil works in the name of Yeshua. Let our leaders not bear the sword in vain but be revengers to execute wrath upon those that do evil in Jesus name. Let the people be law abiding and loving in the name of Yeshua. Let Christians especially be obedient to Your word and obey law and order in Jesus name.

Thank You Lord for helping us. In the name of Yeshua I pray. Amein.

Day 8

Here is a start out prayer based on Psalm 92:1-2, 7-12, 15 and Ephesians 6:10-18.

Our heavenly Father, thank You for Your love, Your mercy, Your grace and Your power. It is a good thing to give thanks unto the Lord, and to sing praises unto thy name, O Most High, to show forth Your loving kindness in the morning, and Your faithfulness every night. Lord, You are upright, You are our Rock, there is no unrighteousness in You.

Father, help Your people in the city of Los Angeles (name the city where you live), the state of California (name the state where you live) and the nation of the United States of America (name your country) to be strong in You and in the power of Your might in Jesus name. Let Your people take up the armor of God so that they may withstand in the evil day in the name of Yeshua. Lord, help Your people, having done all, to stand strong in Jesus name. Let Your people stand therefore, having their loins girt about with truth, and having on the breastplate of righteousness, and their feet shod with the preparation of the gospel of peace in Jesus name.

Abba, above all, help Your people to take the shield of faith, wherewith they shall be able to quench all the fiery darts of the wicked and to take the helmet of salvation, and the sword of the Spirit, which is the word of God, praying always with all prayer and supplication in the Spirit, and watching thereunto with all perseverance and supplication for all saints in the name of Yeshua.

Adonai, Your word says that when the wicked spring as the grass, and when all the workers of iniquity do flourish; it is that they shall be destroyed forever, but You, Lord, are most high for evermore, for Your enemies, O Lord, shall perish, all the workers of iniquity shall be scattered. That is the portion of the enemies of Your people in Jesus name. We decree and declare that the enemies of Your people in Los Angeles, California, and in the USA, perish in Yeshua's name.

Daddy, You will exalt the horn of Your people like the horn of an unicorn, Your people shall be anointed with fresh oil, and our eye also shall see our desire on our enemies, and our ears shall hear the desire of the wicked that rise up against us in the name of Yeshua.

So we praise You Father and give You thanks o Lord in Jesus name. Amin.

Day 9

Here is a start out prayer based on Psalm 123:1-3, Proverbs 3:5-6 and Psalm 145:18-19.

Avinu Malkeinu (Our Father, our King in Hebrew), We come to You and seek Your face like the eyes of a servant look unto the hand of his master, and as the eyes of a maiden unto the hand of her mistress; so our eyes wait upon You LORD our God, until You have mercy upon us in the name of Yeshua.

Unto thee lift I up mine eyes, O Thou that dwellest in the heavens, have mercy on me, have mercy upon us, O LORD, have mercy upon us in Jesus name, have mercy on the city of Los Angeles (name the city where you live), the state of California (name the state where you live) and the nation of the United States of America (name your country) for we are exceedingly filled with contempt.

We choose to trust in You Lord with all our hearts and refuse to lean unto our own understanding in the name of Yeshua. Help us to acknowledge You Lord in all our ways and You shall direct our paths in Jesus name. Of a surety, the Lord is nigh unto all them that call upon Him, to all that call upon Him in truth.

Adonai will fulfill the desire of them that fear Him, He also will hear their cry, and will save them. That is our assurance, Lord, we trust in You and praise You for Your deliverance in the name of Yeshua. Amein.

Day 10

Here is a start out prayer based on Hosea 26:6, Deuteronomy 28:7, Psalm 31:19 and 1 John 5:14-15.

All Merciful One, full of grace and glory, thank You for Your love. Thank You for Your mercies, thank You for Your goodness in the Lord Jesus. Father, once again, we call on You to help us in the name of Yeshua.

We pray that the city of Los Angeles (name the city where you live), the state of California (name the state where you live) and the nation of the United States of America (name your country) will turn to You o God, and keep mercy and judgment and wait on You continually in Jesus name.

Adonai Tz'vaot, cause the enemies of Your people, that rise up against them to be smitten before their face in the name of Yeshua. As Your word declares, our enemies shall come out against us one way, and flee before us, seven ways in Jesus name. Oh how great is thy goodness, which thou hast laid up for them that fear thee; which thou hast wrought for them that trust in thee before the sons of men!

We stand strong in Your love and tender mercies, knowing that You shield us in Yeshua. This is the confidence we have in You that when we ask in Jesus name according to Your will, You hear us and answer our petitions, so Father we trust in Your love and thank You for deliverance in Yeshua's holy name. Amin.

Day 11

Here is a start out prayer based on Mark 10:18, Psalm 66:17, Philippians 4:6-7 and Numbers 6:26.

Heavenly Father, thank You for Your mercies and faithfulness. You alone are good and there is no one like You. We cry out to You with our mouths and Your praise is on our tongues. We cry out regarding the city of Los Angeles (name the city where you live), the state of California (name the state where you live) and the nation of the United States of America (name your country) in Jesus name.

Papa, shower Your mercies upon our cities, states and nation in the name of Yeshua. We refuse to be anxious, but in everything by prayer and supplication, with thanksgiving, we let our requests be made known to You and Your peace, which surpasses all understanding, will guard our hearts and minds through Christ Jesus.

Baba, help us fix everything that is wrong in our cities, states and nation in the name of Yeshua. Lift up Your loving countenance upon us and establish for us Your peace, in the name of Jesus I pray. Amein.

Day 12

Here is a start out prayer based on Jeremiah 32:17, Psalm 27:5, 77:2 and 86:7.

Ah Lord GOD! behold, thou hast made the heaven and the earth by thy great power and stretched out arm, and there is nothing too hard for thee." Father that is the declaration prophet Jeremiah made of You. Since You are the Almighty One, we cry out to You in Jesus name. Concerning our cities, states and nation, Lord we cry out to You.

Abba, we specifically ask You to preserve the city of Los Angeles (name the city where you live), the state of California (name the state where you live) and the nation of the United States of America (name your country) from evil and evil doers in the name of Yeshua. Your word declares that "... in the day of trouble He will conceal me in His tabernacle; In the secret place of His tent He will hide me; He will lift me up on a rock..." We rest in Your word that You conceal Your people and keep them in Jesus name. In the day of trouble, Lord, You will hide Your people in the secret place of Your tent and You will lift us upon a rock in the name of Yeshua.

As King David did in the day of trouble, Father, we seek You, we call on You and stretch out our hands to You for You will answer us in the name of Jesus. Remember the blood of Yeshua and save us for You are All Merciful and Kind.

Thank You Lord for Your loving kindness, in Jesus name we pray. Amin.

Day 13

Here is a start out prayer based on Exodus 34:6-7, 1 Timothy 2:5, Psalm 50:15, Ezekiel 18:23, 2 Corinthians 5:17 and Matthew 9:38.

All Merciful One Who reserves mercy for thousands, we run to You in faith through the only Mediator between God and man, the Lord Jesus Christ. Father, You said to call upon You in the day of trouble, and You will deliver us and we shall glorify You, in obedience to Your word, we call on You today in the name of Yeshua. Save the city of Los Angeles (name the city where you live), save California (name the state where you live) and United States of America (name your country) from destruction in Jesus name.

Lord, You have no pleasure in the death of anyone who dies, You delight in repentance and life, therefore Lord GOD, help our cities, help our states, help our nation to repent and live in the name of Yeshua. Abba, You are the Lord God, You are merciful and gracious, longsuffering, and abundant in goodness and truth, You forgive iniquity and transgression and sin, and make us new creatures in Jesus Christ. Let Your grace flood our cities, states and nation in the name of Yeshua.

Lord of the harvest, send effective laborers into Your ripe harvest in the name of Jesus. Let Your word be spoken and proclaimed boldly to the young and old, weak and strong, male and female in the name of Yeshua.

We thank You for a godly change in the spiritual atmosphere of our cities, states and nation in the mighty name of Jesus, amein.

Day 14

Here is a start out prayer based on Genesis 17:1, Luke 1:37, Hebrews 10:19, John 16:23-24, Matthew 6:13, Psalm 6:4, 85:7, Romans 8:32 and Isaiah 54:17.

Elshaddai, the Strong Breasted One, the Almighty One, the One Who is more than enough, with You, nothing shall be impossible. We run to You in faith through the blood of Jesus and we thank You that You beckon us to ask that our joy may be full. Father and God of our Lord Jesus Christ, we ask that You save Los Angeles (name the city where you live), California (name the state where you live) and United States of America (name your country), from terrorist attacks in the name of Yeshua.

Deliver us from evil o Lord, because of Your unfailing love in the name of Jesus. There are rumors of evil and news of violence and danger, but our hope, trust and confidence is in You o Lord in Jesus name. We are secure in Your love and power and we rest in Your mercies and amazing grace in the name of Yeshua. For You that gave up Your only begotten Son for us, You will freely with Him, give us all things in the name of Jesus.

Father, show us your unfailing love, Lord, grant us Your salvation in the name of Yeshua. We declare the destruction of evil plans against our cities, states and nations in Jesus mighty name! Every weapon fashioned against us will not stand in the name of Yeshua.

Thank You Lord for Your deliverance in Jesus name we pray. Amin.

Day 15

Here's a start out prayer based on 1 Thessalonians 4-5, Romans 1:16 and Isaiah 54:15.

Creator of heaven and earth Whom we have the privilege to call heavenly Father, thank You for Your amazing   grace   and   love. We are grateful to be Fathered by You and cherish the honor to call upon Your name through our Lord Yeshua ha Mashiach.

Yahweh help the body of Christ, Your beloved, be ascertained of their election of God and be strong in preaching the gospel not only in word, but also in power, and in the Holy Spirit, and in much assurance of Your grace in Jesus name. Let Christians in Los Angeles (name the city where you live), California (name the state where you live) and United States of America (name your country), rise up and declare the gospel of Jesus Christ boldy for they are not ashamed of the power of God unto salvation to anyone who believes in the name of Yeshua.

We declare Your promise Lord that "Behold, they shall surely gather together, but not by me: whosoever shall gather together against thee shall fall for thy sake," so everyone against us and the work of the ministry shall fall for our sake in the name of Jesus!

We declare our cities, states and nations for Yeshua! Jesus is Lord in our cities, states and nations in Jesus mighty name. Amein.

Day 16

Here's a start out prayer based on Luke 18:1, Ephesians 3:16-17 and 1 Timothy 4:15-16.

Father, thank You for Your faithfulness and Your mercies that are new every morning. Abba, I ask that as the Lord Jesus instructed, that we, Your people will always pray and not faint. Regarding Los Angeles (name the city where you live), California (name the state where you live) and United States of America (name your country), Father, help us to always pray and not faint in Jesus name.

Strengthen Your people Adonai with might in their inner man by Your Spirit according to the riches of Your glory, that Christ may dwell in our hearts by faith that we will be rooted and grounded in Your love in the name of Yeshua. Let Your love inspire everything we do in Jesus name.

Eternal King of glory, help us to meditate upon Your word, to give ourselves wholly to Your word and to take heed unto ourselves and unto the doctrine, and to continue in them in the name of Yeshua. Father, lead us, keep us and empower us, in Jesus name we pray. Amin.

Day 17

Here's a start out prayer based on Psalm 61:1-3, 91:2-4, 100:3 and 1 John 5:14.

Father, thank You for You are good. You are God and You are the Lord. Hear my cry, O God, attend unto my prayer in Jesus name. From the ends of the earth will I cry unto thee. Like David, Lord my heart is overwhelmed, so I come to You that You lead me to the rock that is higher than I, that Rock is You Lord.

You are my shelter and strong tower from the enemy, regarding Los Angeles (name the city where you live), California (name the state where you live) and United States of America (name your country), Father, help us in Yeshua's name. Help our land to overcome injustice, violence, hatred, abuse and war in the name of Jesus. Help us to yield to Your love, power and peace in the name of Yeshua.

I will say of the Lord, He is my refuge and my fortress, my God, in Him do I trust. Surely He shall deliver me from the snare of the fowler, and from the noisome pestilence.

My God shall cover me with His feathers, and under His wings I shall trust, His truth shall be my shield and buckler in Jesus name. Father let this promise be the portion of Your people in this land in the name of Yeshua.

Father, we know that You are the LORD, and You are God. You made us, we did not make ourselves. We are Your people and the sheep of Your pasture. So help us Lord to obey You, to serve You and please You in Jesus name.

Thank You Lord for hearing our prayer and answering because it is in accordance with Your will in the name of Yeshua. Amein.

Day 18

Here's a start out prayer based on Hebrews 4:16, 2 Corinthians 10:5, 2 Timothy 1:7 and Matthew 18:18.

Father, thank You for the awesome privilege and honor to come boldly to Your throne of grace through the blood of Jesus to obtain mercy, and find grace to help in time of need. Lord, we ask for Your mercy upon Los Angeles (name the city where you live), California (name the state where you live) and United States of America (name your country) in Yeshua's name.

We pray for ourselves, our neighbors, our children and adults, our young and old, our strong and weak and our captive and free in Jesus name. Father, let Your mercy reign in the name of Yeshua! Concerning the wellbeing of our cities, Lord, let Your mercy reign!

We cast down imaginations, and every high thing that exalts itself against the knowledge of God in our lives, and bring into captivity every thought to the obedience of Christ in Jesus name. We cancel every thought of evil for our cities in Yeshua's mighty name.

We say NO to the spirit of violence, division, hatred, injustice and untimely death in the great name of Jesus! We say NO to the spirit of fear, anger, hatred and evil, and loose the spirit of love, power and sound mind in Yeshua's name! We enthrone the Lordship of Jesus Christ in our homes and we ask for His mercies on our streets.

Satan, we bind you and your agents and destroy your plans and purpose for our cities in the mighty name of Yeshua!

Thank You Lord for answered prayers in Jesus name, amin!

Day 19

Here's a start out prayer based on Ephesians 6:10, James 4:7, and 2 Thessalonians 3:3.

Heavenly Abba, thank You for Your daily mercies. Thank You for Your love for us. Thank You for your bountiful grace over our lives. Today I ask that You help us, we your people, those who believe in Yeshua as the Son of God, to be strong in You and in the power of Your might.

I particularly pray for saints in Los Angeles (name the city where you live), California (name the state where you live) and United States of America (name your country) to be strong in You and in Your mighty power in Jesus name.

Father, help Your people to submit themselves to You and resist the devil so he may flee from us in the name of Yeshua. Lord, we know that You are faithful, and You will strengthen us and protect us from the evil one, so we trust in You and trust in Your deliverance for our homes, our cities, our states and our nations in Jesus name." Amein.

Day 20

Here's a start out prayer based on Psalm 118:24, Philippians 4:4, and 2 Chronicles 7:14.

"Father, thank You for today is a day You have made, according to Your word, I choose to rejoice in You and be glad today in Jesus name. In keeping with Your word where You declare that "If my people, which are called by my name, shall humble themselves, and pray, and seek my face, and turn from their wicked ways; then will I hear from heaven, and will forgive their sin, and will heal their land," I humble myself and pray in the name of Yeshua.

I seek Your face Lord for Los Angeles (name the city where you live), California (name the state where you live) and United States of America (name your country) in Jesus name. Help us Lord to turn from our wicked ways, and forgive our sins because of the blood of Jesus.

Heavenly Father, please heal our land, help us to bring to pass in our lives, Your purpose, in the name of Jesus. Help us to bring to pass, Your purpose for our cities and states in the name of Yeshua. Help us Lord in Jesus name, to bring to pass Your purpose in our nation.

Thank You Lord for answered prayers in Yeshua's name. Amin."

Day 21

Here's a start out prayer based on Exodus 34:7, Romans 8:32 and Lamentations 3:25-26.

"Father, thank You for You are the God of mercy. You reserve mercy for thousands, forgiving iniquity, transgression and sin. We ask for Your mercy upon Los Angeles (name the city where you live), California (name the state where you live) and United States of America (name your country) in Yeshua's name.

Show us Your mercy Lord because You are the All-Merciful One. You that spared not Your Own Son, but delivered Him up for us all, You shall, with Him also freely give us all things, so we praise You Lord for Your mercy, provision and protection over our land in the name of Jesus.

Your word declares that You are good unto them that wait for you, strengthen us to wait on You continually Lord, that we may enjoy Your goodness. Thank You Father for answering our prayer in the name of Yeshua. Amein.

Intercessory Prayer for Missionaries

Heavenly Father, I commit missionaries serving You in every continent of the world. I pray particularly for ministers in places that are hostile to the gospel. Help Your servants to declare Your word boldly as they ought to speak in Jesus name. Give them utterance that they may open their mouths courageously, to make known the mystery of the gospel to non-believers in the name of Yeshua.

Elshaddai, supply all the needs of Your servants on the field, all their physical, financial, emotional, psychological and spiritual needs, let them be fully met according to Your riches in glory by Christ Jesus in His wonderful name.

Lord, let Your favor be abundant upon Your missionaries, grant them favor with authorities of the nations and cities where they are and with the local people. As your people walk in godly love and preach Your gospel, let them bear much ministerial fruit, empowering others to come into Your kingdom and furnishing them with tools to make disciples in the name of Yeshua.

Thank You Lord for answered prayers and for sending forth laborers into Your harvest in Jesus name. Amin.

Ephesians 6:19-20, Philippians 4:19, 2 Corinthians 5:18 and Matthew 9:38.

Intercessory Prayer for 5-fold Ministers

Father I commit every 5-fold Minister into Your more-than-capable hands. Help Your ministers to be godly examples to the flock and not lords over God's heritage. Let Your ministers have the mindset of the warning given by apostle James that many should not be masters for masters will receive the greater condemnation, so that they order their ministerial duties with godly fear and integrity in Jesus name.

Adonai, strengthen Your men and women that You've called to be apostles, prophets, evangelists, pastors and teachers, to wait on You and be fully obedient that Your purpose of the perfecting of the saints, for the work of the ministry, for the edifying of the body of Christ, till we all come in the unity of the faith, and of the knowledge of the Son of God, unto a perfect man, unto the measure of the stature of the fullness of Christ, that we henceforth be no more children, tossed to and fro, and carried about with every wind of doctrine, by the sleight of men, and cunning craftiness, whereby they lie in wait to deceive, but speaking the truth in love, may grow up into him in all things, which is the head, even Christ, from whom the whole body fitly joined together and compacted by that which every joint supplies, according to the effectual working in the measure of every part, makes increase of the body unto the edifying of itself in love, may be achieved in Jesus name.

Lord, let ministers minister according to the measure of the gift of Christ in them, without fleshly pride or insecure envy, but confidence in God's word and the Holy Spirit, knowing that they can do all things through Christ Who strengthens them. I use my pastor as a point of contact that our ministers shall fulfill the ministry upon their lives. I pray that they uphold the word and integrity in their lives. I ask that they shall stand, having done all to stand. That they shall speak Your word as Your oracles, in the name of our Lord Jesus Christ.

Papa in heaven, help Your ministers to understand that You have made them gifts to the body of Christ and that they order their steps accordingly in Yeshua's name. Help them to care for Your sheep as watchmen, feeding them Your word and not men's wisdom in Jesus name. Let them manage their time, money and talents wisely remembering that they will give account to You in the name of Yeshua. Help their local members to obey them and submit themselves in Jesus name.

Thank You Father for answering my prayer because it is according to Your word in the name of Yeshua, amein.

James 3:1, Ephesians 4:11-16, 1 Peter 5:3, and Hebrews 13:17

Intercessory Prayer for the Body of Christ

Creator of heaven and earth, Whom we have the awesome privilege to call Father, I come before You in humility, gratitude, praise, joy, and boldness, in the name of Yeshua. I am thankful Abba for this amazing grace You've bestowed upon me to be accepted in Your Beloved through the blood of Your one and only Son, Jesus Christ. Thank You for Your Spirit that baptized me into the Body of Christ, when I heeded the call to make the Lamb of God my Savior by believing in my heart that You raised Jesus from the dead and confessing with my mouth that He is my Lord.

Adonai, I bring the body of Messiah to You, help us to fulfill the good works, which You fore ordained that we should walk in, in the name of Jesus. Let us speak the truth in love, holding unto our Head, even the Lord Jesus Christ from Whom the whole body fitly joined together and compacted by that which every joint supplies, according to the effectual working in the measure of every part, makes increase of the body unto the edifying of itself in love in Yeshua's mighty name. Lord, as we have been built upon the foundation of the apostles and prophets, Jesus Christ Himself being the chief cornerstone Whom all the building fitly framed together grows into a holy temple in the Lord, help us to be continually conscious of the fact that we belong to You and to live our lives to the glory of Your holy name in the name of Jesus.

Baba, imbue us with the knowledge that we are built together for a habitation of You, God through the Holy Spirit, so let us be purposeful in being led by Your Spirit and Your word in the choices we make daily in Yeshua's name. Papa, help Your people to endure hardness as good soldiers of Christ, studying to show themselves approved unto You, as workmen that need not to be ashamed, rightly dividing the word of truth.

Help the body of Christ to be strong in You and in the power of Your might, putting on the whole armor of God that they might stand in the evil day against the wiles, fiery darts and devices of the wicked one and having done all to stand, to stand in faith and assurance of Your word that we always triumph in Jesus name.

Father, teach us daily how to hold the Head, even Yeshua, from which all the body by joints and bands having nourishment ministers, and knit together, increases with the increase of God, that we may fight the good fight of faith effectively, laying hold on eternal life, whereunto we were called and have professed a good profession before many witnesses in the name of Jesus.

I pray for every member of the body of Christ. I pray for babes in Christ that they shall desire the sincere milk of the word and grow thereby, becoming mature in the word, comparing spiritual with spiritual, rightly dividing the word of truth in Yeshua's name. I pray that those of us who are strong in Christ will consider the weak, bearing one another's burden, fulfilling the law of Christ and keeping the spirit of unity in a bond of peace in Jesus name. Adonai, let Your love be expressed in truth and deed among the body of Christ.

I pray for the old in the body that they will enjoy the healing that Jesus purchased for them. I pray for homes in the body of Christ. I pray for peace, love, and joy in homes in Jesus name. I pray that those in financial debt shall be blessed. I declare that their needs are met in the name of Yeshua. I ask that husbands will love their wives as Christ loves the church in Jesus name.

I pray that wives will submit to their husbands as they submit to You in the name of Yeshua. I thank You Abba, for children in the body. I ask that as the Lord Jesus, they shall grow in wisdom, grace, and in stature, having favor with You and with all men. I pray that they will be taught of You and that You will keep them safe. I declare that our children are kept from the evil one in Jesus name.

Daddy, thank You that Your people will be rooted and built up in Yeshua and established in the faith, abounding therein with thanksgiving, and Your intent that the principalities and powers in heavenly places might know Your manifold wisdom through Your church will be achieved in the name of Jesus.

Empower Your called out ones to continually speak to each other in psalms, hymns and spiritual songs, singing and making melody in their hearts to You in Yeshua's name. We worship You Lord, we praise, adore, glorify, magnify and exalt You for answered prayers in the name of Jesus, amein.

---

1 Corinthians 12:13, 2 Corinthians 2:14, Romans 8:14, 10:9-10, Ephesians 1:6, 2:10, 20-22, 3:10 4:3, 15-16, 5:19, Colossians 2:7, 10, 1 Timothy 6:12, 2 Timothy 2:3, 15, I Peter 2:2, Galatians 6:2 and 1 John 3:18.

Intercession for Intercessors

Father, we bring Your watchmen unto You, help them to stand firm in faith and prayer putting on the whole armor of God as they minister to You and stand in the gap for other Christians and non-Christians in Jesus name. Lord as You set watchmen on the walls of Jerusalem, You have raised up watchmen in our time to never hold their peace, but make mention of You, and cry out to You. Strengthen Your intercessors from fatigue, discouragement and lack of direction in the name of Yeshua, for we know that the evil one will attempt to weary them. Let the plans of Satan to steal, kill and destroy Your people come to nought in Jesus name.

Adonai, give Your prayer warriors insight, boldness and unction to root out, pull down, destroy, throw down, build, and to plant in the name of Yeshua. Let every weapon fashioned against them fail in Jesus mighty name. Cause their hearts to be dedicated to You and the gospel, being instant in season and out of season to declare the word and decree your full counsel in the name of Yeshua.

Thank You Father for answering our prayer and establishing Your watchmen and keeping them strong in You in Jesus name, amin.

Isaiah 54:17, 62:6, Ephesians 6:18, Daniel 7:25, Jeremiah 1:10 and 2 Timothy 4:2.

Intercessory Prayer for the Unsaved

Heavenly Father, I pray for those who are not yet saved, I ask that You bring the appropriate minister, a faithful witness of the body of Christ to each unsaved soul regardless of sex, age and nationality in Yeshua's name. I request that the opponents of the cross be gently instructed in the hope that You will grant them repentance leading to a knowledge of the truth in Jesus name. Lord, let these non-Christians come to their senses and escape the trap of the Devil who has taken them captive to do his will in the name of Yeshua.

I declare that the barriers created by the Devil be removed, that there would be no miscommunication in the hearts of these potential believers of Your love and purpose in Jesus name. Adonai, I pray that the light of the gospel of Christ will shine in the hearts of everyone listening to the gospel and that they will understand the good news in the name of Yeshua.

Thank You Lord, for souls that will become saved today, I rejoice with the angels in heaven for these souls in Jesus name. I ask that these new believers will find a Word-obeying church and grow spiritually in the name of Yeshua. All praise, glory, honor to You for Your amazing love to us, in the name of Jesus, amein.

---

2 Timothy 2:25-26, 2 Corinthians 4:4-6, and Luke 15:7-10.

Intercessory Prayers for Broken Homes

Father of Lights with Whom there is no shadow of turning, I come to You in humility and faith asking for Your deliverance for broken homes in the name of Yeshua. Father, You created the family and You love unity, restore broken homes Lord in Jesus mighty name. Let the spirit of Elijah go forth and restore the hearts of the fathers to the sons and the hearts of the mothers to the daughters in the name of Yeshua.

Father, as Elijah repaired the altar of the Lord that was broken, raise up in broken homes, an Elijah that will repair the broken altar of the love of God in the name of Jesus. Bring families together Lord, from the north, the west, the south and the east in the name of Yeshua.

Balm in Gilead, heal every wound, soothe every pain, kill hatred, revive love, grace and power in the mighty name of Jesus I pray. Blood of Yeshua, cleanse, heal, break, tear down, repair build, recreate, establish and settle homes. Thank You Lord for answered prayers in Yeshua's name. Amein.

_____

Malachi 4:6, 1 Kings 18:30, Jeremiah 8:22

Intercessory Prayers for Family Members

Gracious Father of mercy and love, I cry out to you regarding my family members. I pray for my nuclear and extended family members and I ask that Your mercy will be abundant towards us in the name of Yeshua. Lord I pray for those who are not yet saved that You will send Your faithful laborer to share Your gospel with them in a way that their eyes will become enlightened and they will yield their hearts and lives to the gospel of the Lord Jesus Christ in Jesus name.

I pray that Your peace, love and wisdom will reign in my family and ask that members will live honorably and conscientiously, retaining humility, mercy and dignity in their lives in Yeshua's name. Adonai, let Your word be the pillar of my family and let us be known as a family that loves the Lord and obeys His word in the name of Jesus.

Elshaddai, heal every bitterness, envy, hurt, strife and dissension within my family, nuclear and extended, and let Your love empower us to forgive and restitute in the name of Yeshua. Let our family have all sufficiency in all things and be compassionate and generous, let us not be impoverished or ungodly in the name of Jesus.

Adversary, I bind you concerning my household and my extended family members in the name of Yeshua. Take your hands off everyone and everything that belongs to me in Jesus name. I take back everything you've stolen from my family in Yeshua's name. I plead the blood of Jesus over my family members and my extended family in the name of Jesus! No evil shall befall my family members, nuclear and extended in the name of Yeshua! Every weapon fashioned against us will not prosper and every tongue that rises against us is condemned in Jesus name.

Baba, according to Your word, I declare that everyone in my household are saved in Yeshua's name. Papa, I thank You for the salvation of all my extended family members in Jesus name.

Father, I worship and magnify Your holy name that my family shall live for You and glorify You in Jesus name, amin.

---

2 Timothy 2:25-26, 2 Corinthians 4:4-6, 9:8, Luke 15:7-10, Acts 16:31, Matthew 18:18 and Isaiah 54:17.

Intercessory Prayers for Friends

My heavenly Father, I praise You and glorify Your holy name. You are the God of all mercy and grace. I ask for Your mercy and grace upon my friends in the name of Jesus. Help my friends to be people of integrity and righteousness in the name of Yeshua. Since bad company corrupts good morals, Abba, let my friends be godly company, or let them cease to be my friends in Jesus name.

Lord, help my friends cast their burdens upon You for You will sustain them in the name of Yeshua. Quicken my friends to regularly remember that it is You Lord that gives them power to get wealth that You may establish Your covenant, so that they put their trust in You regarding their wealth and their lives in Jesus name.

Abba, cause my friends to shun the temptation to eat the bread of sorrow or walk in the lust of the flesh, but to be conscious of the fact that their bodies are the temple of the Holy Spirit and to yield their members to righteousness and their minds to Your word in Jesus name.

Thank You Lord for helping my friends to dedicate their lives to You and chose to live by Your word in every area of their lives in Jesus name! Amin.

---

1 Corinthians 15:33, Psalm 55:22, 127:2, Deuteronomy 38:18, and Romans 12:1-2,

Intercessory Prayers for Fiends

Heavenly Father, thank You for the awesome privilege to come boldly to Your throne of grace to receive mercy for every time of need. I bring my fiends, my foes, my enemies to You in the name of Yeshua. Father, You desire that all come to repentance so I ask that my fiends who are not saved will become saved in Jesus name.

Lord, I commit every witch, wizard, sorcerer, idolater, occultist, evil man and evil woman to Your merciful hands in the name of Yeshua. Send the perfect laborer to them to remind them that life is short, and they should know the measure of their days, and choose to obey You instead of the evil one in Jesus name. Help them Lord to recognize how frail they are and yield to You, the true God, in the name of Jesus.

Your word says "Rejoice not when thine enemy falleth, and let not thine heart be glad when he stumbleth: Lest the LORD see *it*, and it displease him, and he turn away his wrath from him," and also that "If thine enemy be hungry, give him bread to eat; and if he be thirsty, give him water to drink: For thou shalt heap coals of fire upon his head, and the LORD shall reward thee," so Lord I pray that my fiends will recognize Your judgement upon their lives and submit to Your authority in Jesus name.

According to Your word Lord, I choose not to be overcome of evil, but I overcome evil with good in Yeshua's name. My heart is fixed trusting in You Lord and I shall see my desire upon my enemies in the name of Jesus. Thank You Lord that You contend with my enemies and deliver me from the wicked person in Yeshua's name. I praise You Adonai that You will keep me from the hands of the wicked and preserve me from the violent man who has purposed to overthrow my goings in Jesus name.

Lord of hosts, You will not grant the desires of the wicked but You will maintain the cause of the righteous and afflicted in the name of Yeshua. Thank You that an evil speaker will not be established on the earth and evil shall hunt the violent man to overthrow him in Jesus name. In accordance with Your word, Lord, the rod of the wicked shall not rest upon the lot of the righteous; lest the righteous put forth their hands unto iniquity, yes, wickedness shall not prosper against my life in the name of Yeshua.

Yahweh's word declares that it shall not be well with the wicked, neither shall the wicked prolong his/her days, because they do not fear God, therefore, I pray that my fiends who choose not to fear God shall receive His judgement in the name of Jesus.

"O GOD the Lord, the strength of my salvation, thou hast covered my head in the day of battle. Surely the righteous shall give thanks unto thy name, the upright shall dwell in thy presence." That is Your word Lord and I claim it in Yeshua's name. Thank You Lord for Your faithfulness in Jesus name I pray.   Amin.

_____

Hebrews 4:12, Proverbs 24:17, 25:21, Romans 12:21-22, Psalms 39:4, 92:9-11, 140:1,4,7, 11-13,125:3, Isaiah 49:25 and Ecclesiastes 8:13.

Part 4 - Warfare Prayers

The believer in the Lord Jesus Christ is a soldier! We are called to fight! It is a spiritual war and we have been given spiritual tools which we must use effectively! Our mouth is the main battleship and our words are the ammunition. We MUST declare God's word over our lives and also proclaim His judgment upon evil spirits.

Thou therefore endure hardness, as a good soldier of Jesus Christ. No man that warreth entangleth himself with the affairs of this life; that he may please him who hath chosen him to be a soldier. And if a man also strive for masteries, yet is he not crowned, except he strive lawfully. – 2 Timothy 2:3-5.

For we wrestle not against flesh and blood, but against principalities, against powers, against the rulers of the darkness of this world, against spiritual wickedness in high places. – Ephesians 6:12.

To the intent that now unto the principalities and powers in heavenly places might be known by the church the manifold wisdom of God, - Ephesians 3:10.

In this section I have compiled seven warfare prayers using the *word of God, the name of Jesus, the blood of the Lamb, the fire of the Holy Spirit* and *releasing angels of God* as weaponry. There are many more warfare payers. I recommend the book *101 Weapons of Warfare* by Dr. Daniel K. Olukoya as a good resource.

Be a good soldier, fight the good fight of faith!

Taking Authority over Generational Spirits

Father in heaven, thank You for the blood of Jesus by which I have become Your righteousness. I praise You for whatever I bind on earth is bound in heaven and whatever I loose on earth is loosed in heaven in Yeshua's name.

I know that someone in my ancestry may have practiced sorcery and idolatry and committed unborn children to the control of Satan and the evil one proceeds to exercise this right but halleluYah, Yeshua ha Mashiach (Jesus the Messiah) spoiled principalities, powers and the evil one, so I enforce His victory over my life and my family in Jesus name.

I decree and declare that no generational curse will prosper in my life. I curse bloodline curses and proclaim that they are cancelled in my life and family in the name of Yeshua.

I break any evil covenant in my bloodline, transferring to my life or that of my family in the name of Jesus!

I announce that every evil spirit attached to my generation is powerless over my life and my family because I am in the everlasting covenant of Jesus Christ!

The blood of Jesus has set me free from sin and evil covenants in my bloodline in Yeshua's name.

Every generational curse in my father's house, break by the blood of Jesus in the name of Yeshua.

Every generational curse in my mother's house, break by the blood of Jesus in the name of Yeshua.

I plead the blood of Jesus over my life!

My covenant with Jesus Christ supersedes any other covenant made over my life before I was conceived, before I was born, while I was birthed, and after I was born in the name of Jesus!

The blood of Jesus Christ speaks for me and it is what the blood of Jesus says concerning my life that shall come to pass in Yeshua's name.

Fire of the Holy Spirit, go into my foundation and burn any ungodly covenant, break every evil curse in Jesus mighty name!

Fire of the Holy Spirit, destroy any evil altar containing my name and/or any evil programming against my life in Yeshua's name.

No evil shall befall me in the name of Yeshua and no plague shall come near my dwelling in Jesus name.

I destroy any enchantment, divination, occultic pronouncement, spell, curse, jinx, sorcery, witchcraft and spiritual manipulation assigned against my life in the name of Yeshua.

Every evil writing concerning me in the spiritual realm is cancelled in Jesus name.

No satanic activity against my life will prosper in Yeshua's name.

Iniquity, transgression, sin, infection, genetic anomaly, disease, ailment, sickness, illness, and improper mental disposition orchestrated into my life due to a generational curse or curses, I cancel them all by the blood of Jesus in Jesus mighty name.

Every curse of poverty, affliction, rejection, violence, abuse, demotion, betrayal, profitless labor, hatred and untimely death programmed into my life by generational curses, be destroyed by the fire of the Holy Spirit in the name of Yeshua!

Any strongman, familiar spirit, and spiritual representative assigned to my life due to any generational covenant, I divorce you in the name of Jesus!

Programmed curses and time-based jinxes set to activate and manifest at certain times in my life, be destroyed by the blood of Jesus and the fire of the Holy Spirit in Yeshua's name!

I am free from any and every generational curse in Jesus mighty name!

Father, I praise You and worship you for Your word is honored in my life in the name of Yeshua. I glorify Your name and proclaim Your deliverance in my life. I am more than a conqueror in Jesus name, I triumph always in Christ Jesus. HalleluYAH! Thank You Father, in Yeshua's name I pray. Amein.

Matthew 18:18, Job 5:12-16, Isaiah 48:22, Luke 10:19, 13:16, Deuteronomy 5:9, 28:15-68, Galatians 3:13, 1 John 3:8, Colossians 1:13, 2:15, Hebrews 2:14,12:24, Revelation 12:11, Mark 3:27, Romans 8:37, 1 Corinthians 15:57 and 2 Corinthians 2:14.

Taking Authority over Jealousy &
Vengeful Spirits

My Father in heaven, I honor You and give You praise for You are good and Your mercies endure forever. Thank You for the privilege to utilize the name of Yeshua, the blood of Jesus, the fire of the Holy Spirit, the authority to make a decree and Your word, to fight the good fight of faith in Jesus name.

Father, tongues of jealousy, envy and wickedness have risen against me, I pray that the arrows from these tongues return back to sender in the name of Yeshua.

Any spirit that wants to attack and harass me because I am obeying God's word, become powerless in the name of Jesus!

Vengeful spirits, angry spirits, raging spirits, embarrassing spirits, shaming spirits assigned against my life, STOP in the name of Yeshua and return to your sender in Jesus name!

Destroy, O Lord, the devices of the wicked against me and divide the tongues of the wicked at their gathering when they plot against me in the name of Yeshua!

Every Herod assigned against my life, DIE, in the name of Jesus!

My Father, I run into the name of Yeshua and I am safe from the strife of tongues in Yeshua's name. You hide me from the secret counsel of the wicked, and deliver me from the insurrection of the workers of iniquity in the name of Jesus.

Angels of the living God, arise, return back to sender, every evil arrow fired against me and my family in the name of Yeshua.

It is written, *Associate yourselves, O ye people, and ye shall be broken in pieces; and give ear, all ye of far countries: gird yourselves, and ye shall be broken in pieces; Take counsel together, and it shall come to nought; speak the word, and it shall not stand: for God is with us* – every association of evil concerning my life be destroyed in Yeshua's name.

Every arrow of regression, oppression, bitterness, failure and demotion fired into my life, return back to sender in Jesus name!

Father, release Your warring angels to battle my stubborn pursuers in the mighty name of Jesus!

Every weapon fashioned against my life will not prosper in the name of Yeshua.

Every tongue that rises up against me is condemned in Jesus name.

Where envy and strife is there is confusion and every evil work, envy and strife, cease in my life in Yeshua's name!

Thank You Lord for shining forth Your glory in my life. I arise and shine for Your glory is risen upon me in Yeshua's name. Amin.

Psalm 106:1, Job 22:28, 1 Timothy 6:12, Matthew 2:13-23, Psalm 55:9, Isaiah 8:9-10, 60:1-2 and James 3:16.

Taking Authority over Spirits of Poverty & Hardship

Lord of hosts, I thank You that You desire above all things that I prosper and be in health, even as my soul prospers. I praise You because You delight in the prosperity of Your servants and You supply my every need in Yeshua ha Mashaich. Therefore, Father, I refuse to let the spirit of poverty and hardships rule my life in Jesus name!

Evil spirits or poverty and hardships, I break your power over my life in the name of Jesus!

Elshaddai is the one Who has given me power to get wealth, that He may establish His covenant with me, I bind the spirit of poverty and hardship in my life in the name of Yeshua!

Spirits of poverty and hardship, get out of my finances, get out of my bank account, get out of my paycheck, get out of my business, get out of my home, get out of my career, get out of my mind, get out of my relationships, get out of my family, get out of my workplace, get out of my dreams, get out of my projects in Jesus mighty name!

I loose the spirits of prosperity, abundance, increase, wealth, surplus, blessings and bounty upon my life in Yeshua's glorious name.

I destroy every foundation of poverty and lack in my life by the blood of Jesus!

I shatter any covenant of poverty made over me by anyone living or dead or any that I have made consciously or unconsciously by the blood of Jesus in Jesus name!

Any manipulation of poverty in my life be removed in the name of Yeshua!

Let any platform of poverty in my life be destroyed in the name of Jesus!

Angels of Adonai, go forth and cause my blessings to come to me from the north, the south, the west, the east, the heavens, and the earth in the name of Yeshua!

Hijackers of my virtues, hijackers of my wealth, hijackers of my glory, you will not prosper in the name of Jesus!

Release my virtues, release my wealth, release my glory, NOW, in Yeshua's mighty name.

Let every bullet, arrow, stone, javelin and dust of poverty thrown at me and my family by evil doers return back to them in the name of Jesus!

Poverty and hardship is not my portion, for Yeshua has come that I might have life and that I might have it more abundantly!

I speak forth abundance, I magnetize increase, I receive wealth, I expect glory and I enjoy the good and fat of the land because of the blood of Jesus in the mighty name of Yeshua!

I proclaim to you mountain of poverty and hardship in my life, become a plain, in the wonderful name of Jesus!

Thank You Father for Your word works, amein.

---

3 John 2, Psalm 35:27, Philippians 4:19, John 10:10, Deuteronomy 8:18, and Hebrews 1:14.

Taking Authority over Spirits of Confusion & Delay

Great Judge of all and Sovereign God, I praise You and magnify Your Holy name for You alone are God and there is none like You. You are not the author of confusion but of peace so whatever is bringing confusion into my life is not of You.

I bind the spirits of confusion and delay in my life in the name of Jesus!

Satan, I bind you and your agents from causing confusion and delay in my life in the name of Yeshua.

Every manipulation of evil spirits against my destiny, FAIL, in the name of JESUS!

I speak destruction to every divination and enchantment against me in Yeshua's name.

No conspiracy to cause confusion and delay in my family, ministry, work, dreams and life shall succeed in Jesus name!

I scatter, by the fire of the Holy Spirit, any coven gathering summoned on my behalf, and or on the behalf of my family members in the mighty name of Yeshua!

Warring angels of Adonai Tzva'ot, bring destruction to every tree, crystal ball, padlock, hole, pot, house, cloth, jewelry, dust, amulet, effigy, paper, stone, cup, rock and body parts where witches, sorcerers, warlocks, wizards and other evil agents have programed any evil against me and my family members in the mighty name of Jesus!

Confusion and delay, you will not prosper in my life in Yeshua's holy name.

Agents of confusion and delay in my life be exposed and disgraced in the name of Jesus!

Father, help me to be aware of and properly discern agents of confusion and delay in my life in Yeshua's name.

Lord, reveal to me habits and choices I make that cause or aid confusion and delay in my life in Jesus name.

Abba, equip and empower me to remove from my environment, things and tools that cause delay and confusion in my life in the name of Yeshua.

Power of confusion and delay, cease in my life in the name of Jesus!

Every attack of confusion and delay against me and my family, be defeated in Yeshua's name.

I receive restoration of the years that the locust, cankerworm, caterpillar, and palmerworm has eaten in Jesus name.

I redeem the time for the days are evil and I walk in wisdom towards everyone, especially non-Christians in the name of Yeshua.

Thank You Father for restoring to me everything I have lost due to the activity of the spirit of confusion and delay in Jesus name.

Psalm 86:8, 10, 1 Corinthians 14:33, Philippians 2:9, Colossians 4:5, Ephesians 5:16 and Joel 2:25.

Taking Authority over Spirits of Impatience, Worry, & Fear

Creator of heaven and earth and all therein, Father of the Lord Jesus Christ, Great I am that I am, The Only Wise God, The Almighty, I bow before You, I worship You, I exalt You, I glorify You, I magnify You in Yeshua's holy name.

Father, You have not given me the spirit of fear, but of power, love, and sound mind – so I declare that since fear, worry and impatience, are not from God, they must therefore cease in my life in Jesus name.

Every agent of fear, impatience and worry in my life, be removed in the name of Yeshua.

Worry, fear, impatience, doubt, unbelief and deception, cease in my life by the power of the Holy Spirit in the name of Jesus!

Let the fire of the Holy Spirit burn every amulet, string, metal, parchment, mirror or any other physical tool used as a point of contact by evil spirits and wicked agents to bring and foster worry, fear, impatience, doubt, unbelief and deception into my life and my family in Yeshua's mighty name!

Angels of Adonai, clear away, every evil spirit causing me to fear, worry and become impatient in the name of Jesus!

Power of death and hell, loose your grip over my mind, over my emotions, over my will, over my soul in Yeshua's name.

Arrows of wickedness fired into my brain, eyes, ears, nose, tongue, heart, hands and feet, in order to cause fear, impatience and worry, BACKFIRE in Jesus name!

Every evil covenant made over my life and my family by anyone alive or dead, female or male, young or old, that is activating the programming of fear, impatience and worry into my life, BREAK, and remain broken forever in the name of Yeshua.

I cease to listen to the voice that brings worry, impatience and fear into my life in Jesus name.

I cast down imaginations and every high thing that exalts itself above the reality of God's word in my heart and mind and I bring all my thoughts and imaginations to the obedience of Christ in the name of Yeshua.

God has given me the spirit of love, power and sound mind, I think, say and walk in love, power and sound mind in Jesus name.

According to God's word, His love is shed abroad in my heart by the Holy Spirit, I live in godly love which is patient, so I am patient in the name of Yeshua.

I do not worry about anything but with prayer and supplication, with thanksgiving, I make my requests known to God in Jesus name.

Thank You Father for perfecting Your work in my life in Yeshua's name, amin.

---

2 Timothy 1:7, Revelation1:18, 2 Corinthians 10:5, Romans 5:5 and Philippians 4:7.

Taking Authority over the Spirit of Untimely Death

Father, I repent of any sin I have sinned that opened the door of untimely death to my life in the name of Jesus. Thank You for cleansing me with the blood of Yeshua from all unrighteousness.

In the mighty name of Jesus Christ, I command the spirit of untimely death to desist from my life!

Jesus has died that I may live, His blood has ransomed my life from the grave and He has the keys of hell and death. Death cannot steal my life because my life is hid with Christ in God.

With long life God will satisfy me in Yeshua's name.

I shall not die but live to declare the glory of Adonai in the land of the living. For You Lord has delivered my soul from death, mine eyes from tears, and my feet from falling.

I will walk before the LORD in the land of the living in the name of Yeshua.

Every arrow, bullet, missile, dust, wind, stone, spear of untimely death sent to me, return to your sender in the mighty name of Jesus!

A thousand shall fall at my side, and ten thousand at my right hand, but it shall not come nigh me, only with my eyes shall I behold and see the reward of the wicked.

I cast down imaginations and thoughts of untimely death in the name of Jesus!

Resurrection power of the Holy Spirit, incubate my life in the name of Jesus!

As soon as they hear of me, they shall obey me, strangers shall submit themselves unto me, strangers shall fade away, and be afraid out of their closed places in the name of Yeshua.

Art thou not from everlasting, O LORD my God, mine Holy One? We shall not die, yes O LORD, I shall not die in Jesus name.

The blood of Jesus speaks life for me and its power cancels any evil spoken against me in the name of Yeshua.

(Take communion – eat a small piece of bread and drink a small cup of grape juice in honor of Yeshua's death and resurrection) and declare aloud; "I have eaten the body of Christ, and drank his blood, therefore I have life. Untimely death is defeated in my life in Jesus name."

My outgoing and incoming is blessed of Adonai and no evil shall befall me, neither shall any plague come near my dwelling in Yeshua's name.

Whoever digs a grave for me shall be buried in that grave in Yeshua's name.

No weapon fashioned against me shall prosper and every tongue that rises against me is condemned in Jesus name.

Thank You Lord for Your deliverance in yeshua's mighty name.

Colossians 3:3, Psalm 18:44-45, 91:7,16 116:8-9, 118:17, Habakkuk 1:12, Hebrews 12:24, Proverbs 26:27 and Isaiah 54:17.

Taking Authority over Strange Illness

Most High God and Father of the Lord Jesus Christ, Elshaddai, the Strong-Breasted One Who supplies every need, thank You for making me Your son in Yeshua.

Thank You that my body is the temple of the Holy Spirit and whatever defiles Your temple will be defiled. I speak defilement into this strange illness in my body in the name of Jesus!

Father, I ask for Your forgiveness for any way I opened the door through what I thought, said or did for this illness to come upon me in Yeshua's name.

I curse this illness and command it to die from the roots in the name of Jesus!

I plead the blood of Jesus over my spirit, soul and body in the name of Yeshua.

By the stripes of Jesus, I was healed, I am the healed in Yeshua and I enjoy the healing He purchased for me in Jesus name.

God is pleased when I prosper and when I am in health, I say NO, to anything and anyone stealing, killing and or destroying my health and wealth in the name of Yeshua.

I am in Christ Who lives in Zion and in Zion, none shall be sick!

Every manipulation of witchcraft to place strange illness in my body, my mind and my emotions, be destroyed in Jesus name!

Owner of evil load, carry Your load in the name of Jesus!

Every astral projection, dream projection and evil programming to make me sick, or implant sickness in me, FAIL, in the name of Yeshua!

I destroy every evil altar bearing my name in the mighty name of Yeshua!

O God arise, let all my enemies be scattered in Jesus name!

I destroy the effect of any strange food I have eaten by the blood of Jesus, in Yeshua's name.

Every organ, every cell, every tissue, every system, every fiber in my body functions in the perfection that Yeshua created it to function in the name of Jesus!

Every organ, every cell, every tissue, every system, every fiber in my body is shaped and sized in the perfection that Jesus created it to be shaped and sized in the name of Yeshua!

Angels of the Living God assigned to minister to me are free to minister, they are not hindered in anyway in the name of Jesus!

Warring angels of Adonai, scatter every gathering of evil conspired against me in Yeshua's name.

Every message and messenger of evil against my health, backfire in Jesus name!

Thank You Father for total healing in my body, soul and spirit in Yeshua's name.

---

1 Peter 2:24, 3 John 2, 1 Corinthians 3:16-17, Isaiah 33:24, Psalm 68:1, and Philippians 2:10.

Part 5 - Confessional Prayers

Death and life are in the power of the tongue: and they that love it shall eat the fruit thereof. - Proverbs 18:21.

Confessional prayers, also known as declaring the word of God or personalizing God's promises, or prophetic prayers or proclaiming the word are the building blocks of living an effective and triumphant Christian life.

Philemon 1:6 states; "That the communication of thy faith may become effectual by the acknowledging of every good thing which is in you in Christ Jesus." As we speak forth God's word over our lives we call those things which are not physically there as though they were, and because these things are there spiritually, our declarations actually bring these things from the spiritual realm to the physical realm.

Romans 10:17 - "So then faith *cometh* by hearing, and hearing by the word of God." - Saying out God's word produces faith (Romans 10:6-8) reminds us that the word of faith is in our mouth and hearts and 2 Corinthians 4:13 informs us that the spirit of faith believes and speaks.

In this section there are prayers that must be prayed out loud on healing, professions of faith, who we are in Christ, what we have in Christ, and what we are to do in Christ. An excellent resource on confessional prayers is my book - *Living Words of Prayer*, make sure you have a copy.

"And take ... the sword of the Spirit, which is the word of God." - Ephesians 6:17.

Professions of Faith

I am blessed of the Lord Jesus Christ. I am blessed going out and I am blessed coming in in Jesus name.

Everything I lay my hands to do is blessed in the name of Yeshua.

God my Father ensures that all grace is multiplied unto me, in all circumstances, I have more than enough for every good work and charitable donation in the name of Jesus.

God opens the windows of heaven unto me because I am a faithful tither. I receive open-windows of heaven blessings in a more than enough measure. My vine does not cast her fruit before time and the devourer is rebuked concerning what is mine. All nations call me blessed, and I am always a delightsome land in Yeshua's name.

Because I have given gifts, gifts are given unto me, good measure, pressed down, shaken together and running over do men give to my bosom, purse, and bank account in Jesus name.

God's ministers are free to minister unto me and bring my blessings. They are not hindered in any way in the name of Yeshua.

All my needs are met according to God's riches in glory in Christ Jesus.

I can do all things through Christ Who strengthens me in the name of Yeshua.

I remember the words of my Lord Jesus Christ.

I speak things that become sound doctrine in the name of Yeshua.

I let no man despise my youth, but I am an example of the believers, in word, in conversation, in charity, in spirit, in faith, and in purity, and I give attendance to reading of God's word, to exhortation, to doctrine in Jesus name.

Adonai make me to increase and abound in love toward other Christians and even non-Christians and He establishes my heart unblameable in holiness before Him, and also at the coming of my Lord Jesus Christ with all His saints in the name of Yeshua.

I do not cast away my confidence, which has a great recompense of reward, I am patient so that, after I have done the will of God, I might receive the promise in the name of Jesus.

I am patient and I establish my heart for the coming of the Lord draws nigh in Yeshua's name.

I honor all men, and love the brotherhood. I fear God and honor the king in Jesus name.

God loves me and He sent His Son to be the propitiation for my sins. I love God because He first loved me. Thank You Lord for Your love in the name of Yeshua. Amein.

Deuteronomy 28:6, Psalm 32:1, 2 Corinthians 5:21, 9:8, Malachi 3:10-12 Luke 6:38, 24:8, Philippians 4:13, 19, 1 Thessalonians 3:12-13, 1 Timothy 4:12-13, Titus 2:1, Hebrews 10:35-36, James 5:8, 1 Peter 2:17 and 1 John 4:10, 19.

Confessional Prayer for Healing

According to God's word;

By the stripes of Jesus Christ, I was healed. I am the healed in Christ Jesus. I enjoy the healing that Christ purchased for me. (I Peter 2:24).

.I prosper and I am in health as my soul prospers (3 John 2).

I am an inhabitant of Zion, I have been forgiven my iniquity. I shall not be sick or say that I am sick. (Isaiah 33:24).

I serve the Lord my God, Jesus Christ, He has blessed my bread and water. He has removed sickness from me. (Exodus 23:25).

I am a believer and these signs follow me. I lay my hands on the sick and they recover, I lay my hands on myself and I recover. (Mark 16:8).

Jesus Christ bore my griefs and carried my sorrows; He was stricken, smitten and afflicted on my behalf. He was wounded for my iniquities, He was bruised for my transgressions, the chastisement of my peace was laid upon Him, and by His stripes, I am healed. (Isaiah 53: 4-5). .

In Jesus name!

Amein.

Declarative Prayer for Personal Healing

I take authority over sickness in my body in Jesus name. I declare that every cell, every tissue, every organ, every system in my physical body works as God created it to work. My body is the temple of the Holy Spirit.

I eat right, feel right and live right. I am in the everlasting covenant of Jesus Christ and my covenant with Christ supersedes any natural law of sickness and disease.

I have been redeemed from the curse of the law in Christ Jesus and I enjoy the benefits of redemption in my Lord Jesus Christ in His holy name. Amin!

Mathew 18:18, Mark 16:17, 1 Corinthians 6:19, Galatians 3:13, Philippians 2:10 and Philemon 1:6.

Who We are in Christ

Thank You Father for who You have made me in Christ Jesus. According to Your word, I am complete in Him, Yeshua, Who is the Head of all principality and power, in Whom I am circumcised with the circumcision made without hands and buried with Him in baptism and risen with Him through the faith of the operation of God, Who raised Him from the dead.

I am now the son of God, and I am a new creature, yes, I am God's righteousness in Christ Jesus. I am a chosen generation, a royal priesthood, a holy nation, a peculiar person and I am the redeemed of the Lord, the blood of Jesus has given me redemption even the forgiveness of all my sins, I am of the Day. I am redeemed from the curse of the law, I am delivered from the power of darkness and translated into the kingdom of God's dear son. God loves me, and has given me everlasting consolation and good hope through grace and I have obtained the glory of the Lord Jesus Christ.

I am a good soldier of Christ, I believe in Jesus Christ and I also suffer for Him, I am a partaker of the afflictions of the gospel according to the power of God. I am dead with Christ to the rudiments of the world, I have been given the Holy Spirit, I am appointed to obtain salvation by the Lord Jesus Christ, I am a vessel unto honor, sanctified, and meet for the master's use, and prepared unto every good work. I am purified unto Christ, I am a peculiar person, zealous of good works.

In Christ, I am called a saint, I am a saint, I am holy, unblameable and unreproveable in God's sight, I am sanctified, I am a partaker of the inheritance of the saints in light.

In Christ, I am blessed with all spiritual blessings in the heavenly places, I am God's heir, I am a joint-heir with Christ, I am alive to God, I am a member of the household of God, I am named of God, I am the elect of God, I am holy, I am beloved in Jesus name.

I am the circumcision, that worships God in the spirit, and rejoice in Christ Jesus, and have no confidence in the flesh. God has, from the beginning, chosen me to obtain salvation through sanctification of the Spirit and belief of the truth in the name of Yeshua.

I am a king and priest unto God the Father, I am accepted in the beloved, I am risen with Christ and sited with Him in the heavenly places, I am saved through faith, I am God's workmanship in Christ Jesus, created unto good works that God predestined that I should walk in. I am an able minister of the new testament, not of the letter, but of the Spirit: for the letter kills, but the Spirit gives life, I am an ambassador for Christ, a vessel for godly use. I am a servant of Christ.

Thank You Lord for all You've made me in Christ Jesus. Help me to walk, work and live from the reality of Your word in the name of Yeshua, amein.

Colossians 1:2,12-13, 2:10-12,20 3:1,12, 1 John 3:1-2, 1 Corinthians 1:2, 2 Corinthians 3:6, 5:17, 20-21, Galatians 3:13, Revelation 1:6, Ephesians 1:3,6,11 2:1,6,8,10,19 3:15, 6:6, Romans 1:3, 8:17, Philippians 1:29, I Thessalonians 4:8, 5:8-9, 2 Thessalonians 1:13-14, 16, and 2 Timothy 1:8, 2:3,21.

What We are to do in Christ

Read the following verses - Matthew 4:19, Romans 10:9-10, John 3:16, 1 Corinthians 10:14, 2 Corinthians 3:6, 5:11, 18-20, Colossians 4:5-6, 1 Peter 3:15-16, Ephesians 4:29-32, 5:18, 6:10-18, Hebrews 10:25, 12:14, 1 Timothy 4:11-16 and 2 Timothy 2:14-25, 4:2.

My Lord Jesus said to follow Him and He will make me a fisher of men, I declare that I am a fisher of men for Yeshua. I am an able minister of the New Testament and I fulfil my ministry of reconciliation which I received of the Lord.

Daily, in season and out of season, I preach the gospel of the kingdom, that Yeshua is risen from the dead and faith in Him, and receipt of Him as Lord and Savior brings eternal life. I reprove, rebuke, exhort with all longsuffering and doctrine, I open my mouth and speak when prompted by the Holy Spirit letting my speech be always with grace, seasoned with salt, I know how to answer every man, I walk in wisdom toward unbelievers, redeeming the time and I'm ready always to give an answer to every man that asks me a reason of the hope that is in me with meekness and fear, having a good conscience, sanctifying the Lord God in my heart in Jesus name.

I submit to other Christians in the fear of God, speaking to them in psalms, hymns and spiritual songs, singing and making melody in my heart to the Lord, giving thanks always for all things unto God and the Father in the name of our Lord Jesus Christ. I flee idolatry, I purge myself of striving about words which brings no profit, but only subverts. I follow peace with all men and holiness too in Yeshua's name.

I do not forsake the assembling with other believers in the Lord Yeshua, especially as the day of His return is approaching, but I exhort other Christians and I let them exhort me.

I let no corrupt communication proceed out of my mouth, but that which is good to the use of edifying, that it may minister grace unto the hearers, and I do not grieve the Holy Spirit of God, Who seals me unto the day of redemption. I let all bitterness, wrath, anger, clamor, and evil speaking, be put away from me with all malice and I am kind one to other believers, tenderhearted, forgiving them, even as God for Christ's sake hath forgiven me.

From youthful lusts and all lusts, I flee, but I follow righteousness, faith, charity, peace, with them that call on the Lord out of a pure heart. I avoid foolish and unlearned questions knowing that they gender strife, and I, the servant of the Lord must not strive, but I must be gentle unto all, apt to teach, patient, in meekness instructing those that oppose themselves in the name of Yeshua, knowing the terror of the Lord, I persuade men.

I study to show myself approved unto God, a workman that needs not to be ashamed, rightly dividing the word of truth. I shun profane and vain babblings, for they will increase unto more ungodliness and the words eat as a canker, I depart from iniquity and purge myself so I shall be a vessel unto honor, sanctified, and meet for my Master's use, and prepared unto every good work in Jesus name.

I am strong in Adonai, and in the power of His might. In my daily job, I am as a servant of Christ, and I do the will of God from the heart, with good will doing service, as to the Lord, and not to men.

I meditate on God's word and give myself wholly to it that my profiting may appear to all. I take heed unto myself, and unto the doctrine, and I continue in them, for in doing this, I shall both save myself, and them that hear me in the name of Yeshua.

I command and teach the full counsel of God's word and I do not allow anyone to despise my age or sex, but I am an example of the believers, in word, in conversation, in charity, in spirit, in faith, in purity. I give attendance to reading of God's word, to exhortation, to doctrine, and I do not neglect the gift of the Holy Spirit but I am filled continuously with the Spirit of the Living God.

Having done all to stand, I stand therefore, putting on the whole armor of God, that I may be able to stand against the wiles of the devil, and withstand in the evil day, for I wrestle not against flesh and blood, but against principalities, against powers, against the rulers of the darkness of this world, against spiritual wickedness in high places.

I stand therefore, having my loins girt about with truth, and having on the breastplate of righteousness, and my feet shod with the preparation of the gospel of peace, and above all, I take the shield of faith, wherewith I shall be able to quench all the fiery darts of the wicked. And I take the helmet of salvation, and the sword of the Spirit, which is the word of God, praying always with all prayer and supplication in the Spirit, and watching thereunto with all perseverance and supplication for all saints in the name of Jesus.

Thank You Father for helping me to do that which You have predestined me to do in the name of Yeshua I pray, amin.

What We have in Christ

Most Merciful God and Father of the Lord Jesus Christ, thank You for Your love in giving Your only begotten Son to save my soul. Thank You for blessing me with all spiritual blessings in heavenly places in Christ Jesus, yes, You daily load me with benefits, I praise You, God of my salvation for giving me eternal life and giving me access to You and making me part of your beloved.

I am grateful for Your covenant with me through the blood of Yeshua, yes, I have been made near to You and You have given me sonship, I have righteousness, stewardship, priesthood and kingship. I am in an everlasting covenant with You, even as declared through prophet Isaiah, "As for me, this *is* my covenant with them, saith the LORD; My spirit that *is* upon thee, and my words which I have put in thy mouth, shall not depart out of thy mouth, nor out of the mouth of thy seed, nor out of the mouth of thy seed's seed, saith the LORD, from henceforth and forever."

Thanks be to You God for giving me victory through the Lord Jesus Christ, and You always lead me in triumph in Him. I rejoice in You always and I have Your word to live by and declare to others and to Satan and His agents. I have Your armor and I have the name, and the blood of Yeshua. You have also blessed me with the blessed Comforter, the Holy Spirit Who lives in me and guides me and energizes me to pray after Your will in Jesus name. Thank You Lord!

Ephesians 1:3,6, 2:13, Psalm 68:19, John 1:12,3:16, Isaiah 59:21, Matthew 24:45, 1 Peter 2;9, 1 Corinthians 15:57, 2 Corinthians 2:14, 5:21, Ephesians 6:10-18, and Romans 8:26.

A Final Word

Dear reader and praying saint. I'm so glad you've used the prayer helper to pray. Share it with your friends who are saved and use it as an evangelistic tool for those who are not yet saved. Buy copies and give as gifts, you will be winning a soul (Proverbs 11:30).

Whenever you feel overwhelmed, tired, uneasy, angry, sad, embittered or determined, use the Prayer Helper to pray. Don't settle for any ungodly reason as an excuse not to pray. Help yourself to pray, make yourself pray, train yourself to pray.

Prayer is a must and God is ready to help you by His Spirit. Make the word of God your life, daily read the word and pray the word. Use This *Prayer Helper* to help yourself to pray.

You can write me at derbrah@yahoo.com and visit www.adonailove.com, http://livingwordsofprayer.com and http://derbrah.com for more information. If you wish to make a donation you can send it via paypal to derbrah@yahoo.com or send a check to P. O. Box 1054, Loma Linda, CA 92354.

Adonai bless and keep you, Adonai cause His face to shine upon you and be gracious to you, Adonai lift up His loving countenance upon you and establish for you, His peace, bashem Yeshua (in the name of Jesus), amein.

S H A L O M

Continue in prayer, and watch in the same with thanksgiving;
- Colossians 4:2

- Philippians 4:6-7
Be careful for nothing; but in everything by prayer and supplication with thanksgiving let your requests be made known unto God. And the peace of God, which passeth all understanding, shall keep your hearts and minds through Christ Jesus.

1 Thessalonians 5:17 Pray without ceasing.

Romans 12:12 Rejoicing in hope; patient in tribulation; continuing instant in prayer;

Acts 2:42 And they continued stedfastly in the apostles' doctrine and fellowship, and in breaking of bread, and in prayers.

But the end of all things is at hand: be ye therefore sober, and watch unto prayer.
- 1 Peter 4:7

Other Books by Derbrah

With over 217 verses of personalized promises of God's word, *Living Words of Prayer* will equip the believer with godly words to proclaim daily.

Living Words of Prayer

Bless me Daily contains over 300 verses and 30 prayers that parents can use to bless their children daily and train them in the way of the Lord, so they grow godly.

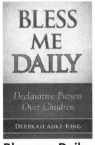

Bless me Daily

Daily Speech is Derbrah's first confessional. It is a tool for the believer to proclaim God's word in a personalized fashion. This book will strengthen the believer's walk with God.

Daily Speech

Audio Books by Derbrah

Living Words of Prayer is recorded on 2 CDs and available as a voice-alone recording;

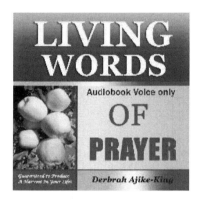

and as a recording with music in the background.

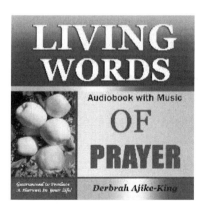

Both serve to assist the listener to pray effectively.

Get your copy!

- 1 Peter 3:12

For the eyes of the Lord *are* over the righteous, and his ears *are open* unto their prayers: but the face of the Lord *is* against them that do evil.

Saying with a loud voice, Worthy is the Lamb that was slain to receive power, and riches, and wisdom, and strength, and honour, and glory, and blessing.

– Revelation 5:12.

Made in the USA
Columbia, SC
24 September 2024

42983663R00059